G

U

OF THE OLD WEST

N

S

Also by Jeff Cooper
Art of the Rifle
Art of the Rifle, Special Color Edition
C Stories
Custom Rifles
Fighting Handguns
Fireworks
Handguns Afield
Jeff Cooper's Defensive Pistolcraft Tape Series
Principles of Personal Defense
To Ride, Shoot Straight, and Speak the Truth

Guns of the Old West
by Jeff Cooper

Foreword copyright © 2008 by Thell Reed
Originally published by Trend Books
Paladin reprint edition 2008

ISBN 13: 978-1-58160-682-9
Printed in the United States of America

Published by Paladin Press, a division of
Paladin Enterprises, Inc.
Gunbarrel Tech Center
7077 Winchester Circle
Boulder, Colorado 80301 USA, +1.303.443.7250

Direct inquiries and/or orders to the above address.

Visit our website at www.paladin-press.com

FOREWORD

I was just a teenager when I first met Jeff Cooper in 1957, while competing in the Leatherslap pistol match at Big Bear Lake, California. After that, I was a regular participant in that annual match and others he ran in the late 1950s. Jeff had a huge influence on my life in so many ways; he was a wonderful teacher of shooting, history, and life. I always found his opinions to be grounded in reality.

Jeff was a genius, a lot smarter than the rest of us. And by us I mean those of us who were close friends and regular visitors to the Cooper home, including Elden Carl, Jack Weaver, Ray Chapman, and me. After spending the day shooting, I thought it was the greatest thing in the world to sit down to dinner with the Cooper family, Jeff and Janelle and their three girls, and later sit back and listen as Jeff talked about shooting, hunting, sports cars, and history. He could describe ancient battles in detail, and each time he talked about a specific battle—even years later—the facts didn't change. He always got it right, and he always told it the same way.

Jeff Cooper was on the cutting edge of combat shooting and firearms development. He was developing the Modern Technique of the Pistol at the time, along with all kinds of other things that shooters today take for granted, such as making sensible fighting modifications to the 1911: enlarging the safety, bobbing the hammer to eliminate hammer bite or replacing it with a Commander hammer and adding a long tang, and installing S&W revolver adjustable sights. The matches and other shooting events that he participated in, like the hunting trips he took around the world, were helping him to develop the Bren Ten pistol (Jeff considered the .40 caliber to be the optimum cartridge—the Old West pistolero John Wesley Hardin had used pistols in that .40-caliber range, and Jeff thought it was the way to go too) and the Scout Rifle, which he played around with for years before he was satisfied with the design. Such matches as the Leatherslap and the Colt Championship Fastest Draw Alive competition (held one time only), which everybody shot with single-action revolvers and live ammunition, set the stage for action pistol competition in this country. Until then, the only action-style pistol matches were either police pistol competition or cowboy fast draw.

When I was older, I joined the Marine Corps (Jeff had been a Marine) and later on I went into the movie business. I'm still in the movie industry as an armorer and a shooting coach for countless movie actors.

CONTENTS

ACKNOWLEDGEMENT—The author and publisher wish to express
their appreciation to Dr. Richard K. Horton of Santa Ana for his
cooperation in photographing his famous gun collection for inclusion
in this book. His is one of the outstanding collections in the country.
He recently turned down an offer of $6,000 for Sam Walker's famous
Colt Walker which he owns and is pictured herein.

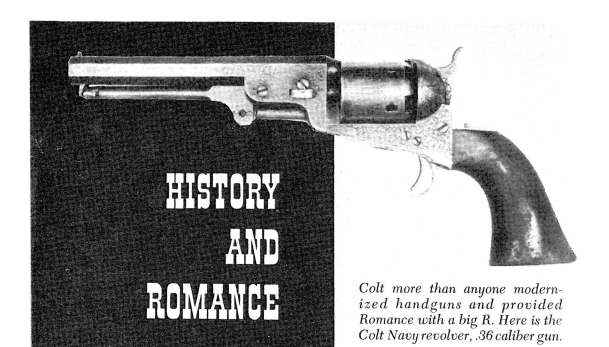

HISTORY AND ROMANCE

Colt more than anyone modernized handguns and provided Romance with a big R. Here is the Colt Navy revolver, .36 caliber gun.

THE romance of the American frontier holds a fascination that seems out of proportion to its importance in the historical scheme of things. The "western" is the most dependable and durable form of entertainment known— the reason for which would be more obvious if it applied only to Americans, but it happens to be true of the entire world! In English country towns, in the suburbs of Helsinki, in Yugoslav mountain villages, and in the oddly-scented playhouses of Upper Burma, stories of the American West maintain a steady popularity unaffected by the shrill vituperation of the Commies or the changing fortunes of the cold war.

Highbrows deplore this mass taste (ignoring the occasionally brilliant efforts in the field) but fact remains— nearly everybody likes westerns. The quality of such an extensive medium naturally varies a great deal, and plots run from childish "good guys vs. bad guys" items to extremely complicated psychological soul struggles, but a few things remain constant—the locale, the horses, and the guns. The country is big, open and free. The horses indicate the

A beautiful suit of armor became junk when firearms came along.

historic period and emphasize the feeling of distances unbridgeable in moments. And the guns—death in a man's hand—bring home the sense of immediate drama that is essential to strong entertainment. When everybody wears a gun, serious arguments are settled conclusively. The loser isn't just embarrassed, or roughed up, or out of a job. He's *dead.* Thus the classical denouement is really a "moment of truth" which never fails to grip the imagination of young or old, man or woman, hick or sophisticate.

The guns which play so vital a part in the matter are the subject of this booklet. Specifically the handguns — the pistols and revolvers which men carried with them in order to be able to step instantly into the role of judge, jury and executioner on an instant's notice. They come in various types and sizes, depending upon the year, the tactical situation, and sheer chance. But they are all objects of interest and allure to those who love the tradition of the old west.

The single pistol has its place in history, but the revolver is the handgun of legend. This is so true that it is actually a handicap today. The semiautomatic pistol is a considerably more efficient sidearm, but we Americans just love revolvers!

However, in order to appreciate the sixgun fully it's necessary to absorb a little background, so a bit of history is in order.

Some say the Chinese invented gunpowder but didn't understand its use as a ballistic propellant. More recent research suggests that its actual discovery took place in Medieval Europe, and that its application to missile weapons was appreciated at once. The match-ignited

cannon was the first true firearm, maintaining its basic form for several centuries—and the little ones, mounted on the end of a staff, were probably the first ancestors of the pistol.

The term "pistol" is often ascribed to the Italian town of Pistoia, where we have evidence that handguns were built as early as 1540. However, special cavalry troopers in Germany used fire from one-hand firearms at the battle of Renty in 1544 and won a significant victory. Four years is just not long enough for a weapon to be invented, perfected, standardized, promoted, sold, and then used to equip large formations trained in its use and employing tactics based entirely upon it. Even if it could have happened, one cannot believe that the town's name, rather than that of the inventor, the troops who used it, or some more descriptive term, would have stuck permanently as the universal name of the weapon.

A better hypothesis holds that the word comes from the Renaissance Italian term for the pommel of a saddle, which is "pistallo." Since the purpose of the earliest pistols was to enable mounted men, who had only one hand free, to use a firearm, they were always carried slung over a saddle pommel, and might very well be named for this fact.

Regardless of the origin of the name, the pistol first appears as a replacement for the lance or sword as the cavalryman's assault weapon. The distance at which a foeman can be reliably hit with a pistol bullet when the shooter is mounted on a galloping horse is extremely short. Anyone who has run the old mounted pistol course of the U.S. Army knows that the best way to get hits is almost to touch your target with the muzzle as you fire. So a question arises

Wheellock pistol.

about what advantage a pistol has over a sword, or especially a lance, in a cavalry action. The answer appears to be that a pistol ball, while somewhat less accurate than a sword or lance thrust when delivered from the upper deck of a running horse, cannot be deflected since it cannot be seen. Also, it may hit harder if a heavy load is used.

At the battle of Renty, the Germans used the ancient alternating-rank system to sustain shock effect, and carried as many as four long-barreled, all-steel, wheellock pistols. But during the centuries which preceded the invention of the repeating pistol it was more customary to fire one round carefully just before matters became hand-to-hand, and then to use cold steel, reserving your other pistol for later emergencies. This system worked well since if the enemy's entire front rank was cut down just before impact the force of a charge was much greater. It's obvious that if each of your men accounts for just one of the enemy and remains in action, you have won your battle.

Military commentaries indicate that the edge of the pistol over the sword and lance for cavalry use was never entirely accepted until just before cavalry left the military scene. While Custer's men at the Little Big Horn had left their sabers behind, there are many to this day who believe that they might have cut their way out if they had brought them along. An empty pistol is no match for a tomahawk, but a saber is something else again!

But while the generals were trying to decide about the capabilities of the sidearm as the horseman's main weapon, other uses for it developed. The single-shot pistol, in spite of its now-or-never limitations, took a lot of the fun out of banditry, bullying, rapine, pillage and other sports enjoyed by the physically strong at the expense of the weak since the Stone Age, and presumably even before that. Suddenly it became actually risky to push people around, even if you stood 6'5", dressed in armor, and carried a battle-axe. Some aged merchant or choice damsel might quite easily blow your head clean off with a little gadget you hadn't noticed at all.

It wasn't really an "equalizer" because, after that one round, everything slipped back into its primeval relationship, but it was a start. And a bully seldom has any notion of getting killed just so his friends can enjoy the loot.

The handgun passed through the same mechanical stages as other guns of all sizes. If pistols are firearms which can be aimed and fired with one hand, they did not exist in "touch-hole" form since the non-pointing hand must put the match to the priming train. "Matchlock" pistols, however, were produced. Their usefulness was never really established, since it depended entirely upon adequate foreknowledge of combat. The matchlock is simply a system by which a lighted fuse (or "match") may be thrust into the priming train with the same hand that holds the weapon. It still must be lighted shortly before discharge, and if you know there's going to be a fight, you can usually equip yourself with something better than a matchlock pistol. A matchlock musket, for instance.

Wheellock pistols were really practical, though they were subject to all the exasperating unreliability of a modern cigarette lighter. It was just a short step

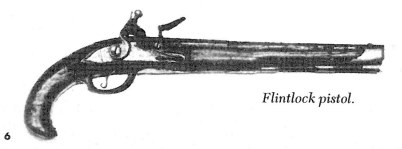

Flintlock pistol.

from the wheellock to the flintlock, which brings us almost up to the present day. The flintlock was neater and simpler than the wheellock, and with its appearance armorers began searching for the next step, a pistol which could keep on shooting and permanently alter close quarter tactics.

Flintlock revolvers can still be found in museums, but the complexity of a priming train for each chamber made them less than practical. As early as 1664, an English inventor tried to interest the Royal Society in a pistol which would use part of the force of discharge to reload, reprime, and recock – probably the first attempt at a semi-automatic pistol. But all such notions had to wait for an ignition system far superior to the crude flint-and-steel which was all that science could offer at the time.

The answer came from a Scottish clergyman, Alexander John Forsyth, who, in 1807, invented the percussion cap. Forsyth did not invent fulminates,

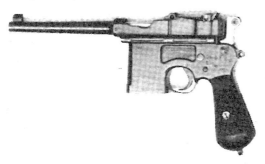

Royale auto pistol, 7.63 Mauser type. Rapid fire gun which lacks heavy punch.

Union Switch and Signal model 1911A1, .45 ACP. Browning-designed pistols are perhaps the finest handguns in the world.

which were known prior to 1700, but he was first to apply them to the ignition of firearms. The percussion cap made all the difference, because it made the ignition system of firearms simple, reliable, compact and capable of being incorporated into moving mechanisms without loss of efficiency. It made possible Sam Colt's revolver which, in the literal, immediate sense, made all men equal. For the first time in history one man was as good as another!

So, while in other lands the toy pistol, the high-velocity, small-bore, "substitute rifle," and the rifle-accurate target pistol were developed, it was in America alone that the lightning-action holster gun, capable of delivering a crushing, man-stopping blow at short range and upon exactly no notice, came into existence.

Compare for a moment the 1898 "broom-handle" Mauser auto pistol and its contemporary, the 1871 Colt "Peacemaker." The Mauser is a magnificent piece of engineering, ingeniously assembled by interlocking parts without pins or screws. It fires a tiny, .30 caliber, jacketed bullet at velocities which were fantastically high for the handguns of its day. It was normally carried in a wooden case which could be fixed to its grip as an auxiliary stock, and its rear sight was adjustable to ranges of 1000 meters. It was, and is, a fascinating collector's item, but as a combat pistol it is a joke. If you want a collapsible carbine good for jackrabbits at 100 yards it's a good gun, but that's *not* what you need a pistol for.

The Colt, on the other hand, fires six huge, heavy, lead slugs at a moderate speed. They don't move too well out beyond 50 yards, but pistols are used in much closer than that. It slips easily out of the leather and points where you look. It rides safe and ready on your hip and cocks instantly on the draw. Given approximately equal ability and courage, the western Colt-packer could face a European officer with a Mauser at his belt and laugh him out of town. The real combat pistol is an American monopoly.

The Man who made all Men equal

THERE have always been those whose chief aim is the destruction of traditional beliefs, without any apparent effort to evaluate the merit or truth of such beliefs. Such people often try to "debunk" Sam Colt as just another gunmaker, but somehow they never succeed. You can call Colt many unflattering things—patent thief, sharp trader, dog-in-the-manger, obstacle to progress, suborner of officials, and such—but you can't shake his position in American history. He *did* produce the Paterson pistol. He *did* create the Walker, the Dragoon, and the 1860 Army. Colt revolvers *did* change both the military tactics of his time and the relationship of a lone man to a hostile environment. No matter how many competitive claims you unearth, you can't change the facts.

The number of people who equate "Colt" with "pistol" is not due merely to smart promotion, though there was plenty of that. The eminence of the Colt name rests squarely on the revolutionary concept that one man is as good as another. Philosophers and politicians worked out this idea toward the beginning of recorded history but it was never *really* true prior to the appearance of the repeating pistol. The legal and constitutional precepts of society mean nothing when one is confronted by an armed foe.

Being within one's rights is cold comfort when a dangerous adversary offers violence. The law will protect the just, but it can arrive too late. However, a sound sidearm—an equalizer—is something on which a man can depend. And Sam Colt put the equalizer on the market.

Colt's contribution was the adaptation of Forsyth's cap lock to the revolver principle. This combination of two established ideas was a case of the whole's being greater than its parts, for Colt's revolver made history in a way no previous individual invention ever did.

Colt was an extraordinarily vigorous and enterprising man—a real hustler. While his inventions were good, his business sense, aggressive promotion, and organizing ability were even better. No sooner had he satisfied himself that his revolver was practical, than he set about protecting it with a detailed set of iron-clad patents which gave him a practical monopoly in the field. Colt's revolver was an improvement over anything else at the time, since his action used the cocking motion of the hammer to rotate and lock the cylinder. This innovation made the revolver a real combat tool, since previous designs required separate locking or rotating actions. His patents sewed up the revolver business tight for decades and he made himself a fortune, as he intended and certainly deserved.

Colt's first patents were granted in England in 1835 and in the U.S. in 1836, when he was just 21 years old. Thus armed, he promoted a corporation, the Patent Arms Manufacturing Company of Paterson, New Jersey, and started turning out guns in the same year. The Paterson factory produced revolving weapons of all types—pistols, rifles, muskets, carbines and shotguns. All used the patented breech system, all were percussion ignited, and all loaded from the front of the cylinder. They were thus not exactly muzzle loaders, though they were in principle, using loose powder, ball and caps for ammunition.

The most prominent piece produced at Paterson, however, was what we call today the "Paterson Colt," the pistol which made Sam Colt's reputation.

The "Paterson" was a curious weapon, and was never really standardized. It was made in .28, .31, .34 and .40 caliber and in each case all the parts were of different sizes. That is, you couldn't simply mount a different barrel and cylinder and produce the next size gun. In the small calibers the Paterson was probably not especially effective, but the .40 caliber version made itself known very quickly as a serious sidearm. All the Patersons had octagonal barrels, five-shot cylinders, folding triggers which sprang out as the hammer was cocked, and a rear sight cut in the top of the hammer. The first models had plain barrels, but in 1839 a hinged rammer lever was permanently attached beneath the barrel. There was no support for the barrel above the cylinder, as on modern revolvers, and the action was quite complicated, involving 17 moving parts. The piece was designed to fire a round ball only and the twist of the rifling was so slow as to be nearly imperceptible. As these pistols came in various sizes you can't give general specifications for them. The biggest one, however, was a medium-sized weapon by modern standards. With a seven-inch barrel it ran 12 inches overall and weighed something over two pounds. All these revolvers were furnished in a handsome case with a five-charge loading tool, a bullet mold, cleaning equipment, and two spare cylinders which could be carried loaded, giving the user 10 more shots after a slight delay, for cylinders could be exchanged in just about the time required to reload a single-barreled muzzle-loading pistol.

The Paterson Colt was never an official arm of any government, and was never produced on contract, but it became instantly popular in Texas, where there was a good deal of fighting at the time, both with Indians and Mexicans. Practically all of the .40 caliber Patersons ended up in Texas and the pistol later became widely known as the "Texas Arm." It was with these guns that Colonel Hays of the Texas Rangers, with 14 men, dispersed a force of 80 Comanches, leaving 33 dead on the field.

Patersons also did well in Florida during the Seminole Wars, and by the outset of our war with Mexico nearly every officer in the U.S. forces who had seen any actual combat was sold on Sam Colt and his guns. But Colt, himself, was in trouble.

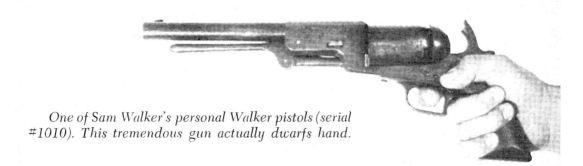

One of Sam Walker's personal Walker pistols (serial #1010). This tremendous gun actually dwarfs hand.

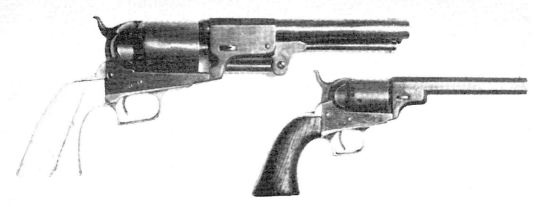

Colt Dragoon is seen at top, with a "Baby Dragoon" below it.

The Paterson Company went bankrupt in 1841, for a number of reasons. The guns were made largely by hand and thus expensive. Most of the country was at peace and didn't really need a repeating sidearm. There was a widespread suspicion of their complexity, and an unfounded belief that the mechanism was unreliable in hard use. (It's always easy to claim that a given machine will break down under certain hypothetical conditions. Since only actual service over a long period proves anything, you can look wise and claim it won't work without having to think much about it.) But probably the real reason the Paterson Company failed was the technical difficulty of getting enough of the guns to the markets which required them so that their real worth could be discovered by the public.

When the factory shut down Colt was left with nothing but his patents. With wisdom unusual in so young a man, he had secured his personal ownership of them when the company was formed. But he forgot about pistols for the time, and set about producing marine mines. When the Mexican War began to loom, he didn't even own a gun to use as a model for any new production.

But down on the border, Zachary Taylor's troops were getting set for trouble. All the Colts that could be found anywhere were procured and issued, but there were not nearly enough, and none

had been made for three years. It was the custom to equip each trooper with two pistols, so 1000 actives needed 2000 Colts.

So there was no place at all for the war-threatened army to obtain the most efficient weapon of its day—except Sam Colt himself, a young man of 30 without money, factory, tools or corporate backing!

Taylor's agent was Captain Samuel H. Walker of the Rangers. In 1846, when his ranger company was integrated into the army, he was 29 and had seen plenty of combat in actions against the Creeks, Seminoles, and Comanches. He was one of Hays' patrol which shot up the 80 Comanches, and he knew all about the use of Sam Colt's tools in a fight. Taylor sent Walker back home to Maryland in the fall of '46 to recruit and also to procure, in some fashion, one thousand Colt revolvers. He found Colt in November and, though there was no apparent means of producing anything, the two men concluded an oral deal. How much influence Walker had on the design of the pistol to be manufactured is debated by historians. The specific improvements in the resulting weapon were great, and definitely reflect the experience of an intelligent, battle-wise officer, but whether they were Walker's own ideas or the combined opinion of Taylor's staff is not known. However it was, Walker delivered the message, and the pistol is known to history as the "Walker Colt."

It's a huge, heavy, powerful weapon—superior in range, hitting-power and accuracy to anything seen before. Its bore size was .44" (a figure reached by the Army's specifying 50 round balls to the pound). It was designed to take either a round ball or a conical bullet, giving it two missile weights—140 and 219 grains. Its long cylinder held *fifty* grains of black powder, and its nine-inch round barrel allowed plenty of time for this mighty charge to start the bullet on its way. While chronographs were not available for consultation, a little study will give you an idea of the pistol's performance. The last factory figure for a black powder load in a .45 Colt was 40 grains of fuel and 250 grains of lead. This produced 910 f/s—a rugged load! But the Walker took 10 grains more powder and 31 grains less bullet, and had four inches more barrel to work in. It should have got well over 1000 f/s with its heavy bullet, and probably was exceeding 1500 with its round ball! This is more muscle than anything we have today except the .44 Magnum. Whoever specified this load wanted to make sure that when he shot a man he wouldn't have to do it again. Walker wrote that the pistol which took his name was as effective as the regular rifle at 100 yards and superior to a musket at 200.

To hold all this power took a lot of metal, since steels in the 1840's were not what they are today, and the Walker was not dainty. It measured 15½ inches overall and weighed in at 73 *ounces,* close to double the ordinary heavy-duty sidearm of today. While this made it cumbersome, it did a lot to soak up the recoil of the heavy load, and since it was the day of the horseman the extra weight was not significant.

There were other improvements, too. The Army wanted six shots instead of the Paterson's five, so the six-shooter was born. Colt himself simplified the lockwork from 17 to five working parts, both to facilitate production and to make a more rugged mechanism. (The action is practically identical with that used today in the Colt Single Action Army and Great Western Frontier pistols.) And the complex and delicate folding trigger of the Paterson was replaced with a straightforward stationary trigger in a square-backed guard.

On the negative side, the hammer notch rear-sight and open-top frame of the earlier pistols were retained, as indeed they were on all revolvers produced by Colt during his lifetime.

But while details of design were agreed upon, and even a unit price ($25 per gun, $3 for each set of accessories), there was still no way to get into production. Colt solved this by taking his project to Eli Whitney in Connecticut, who was producing muskets for the Army, and arranging to build his thousand revolvers in Whitney's plant with Whitney's workmen. This was a workable solution, but in order to build the guns for a price the Army would pay and still give Whitney his share of the profits, Colt had to forego any financial reward for the operation. In fact, he claimed he lost money on the 2000 Walkers made at Whitneyville, but by the time the second order was completed he had the machinery necessary for further production, plus the reputation made by his new arms in actual service, so he packed his tools off to his own new plant at Hartford and was at last in business for himself. All this was done in less than a year, for Walker contacted Colt in November of 1846 and the Hartford plant was open and running in October of '47.

Colt was not satisfied with the Walker pistols because they were made in a rush by workmen unfamiliar with the task. His principle of completely interchangeable parts violated, and the standards of finish and workmanship were not up to what he felt they should be. He also got in trouble with the government because of a misunderstanding about accessories.

He held that one set of accessories for each two guns was understood, as the weapons were always issued in pairs. Ordnance insisted on a complete set for each gun, at the same price. A small matter perhaps, but not to Colt who was operating on a shoestring in order to establish himself.

The Walker Colt was made only at Whitneyville and only in connection with the two 1000-unit orders initiated by Walker, so it's rare today. (A good one brings $3000–$3500.) As soon as Colt was set up in his own plant he recommended a few changes to the Army, which were accepted, and the "Dragoon" Colt supplanted the Walker.

The Dragoon was in production from 1848 clear up until 1860, and therefore is found in many forms with numbers of minor variations. It is quite similar to the Walker, differing principally in that it carries a shorter cylinder in the same length frame, leaving a noticeable gap in front of the cylinder where the Walker is flush. It also usually has a shorter barrel (7½″) and an improved latch to hold the rammer to the barrel. Later models featured a round-back trigger guard and were made to take a detachable shoulder stock.

It was necessary to fit a folding leaf auxiliary rear sight on the rear of the barrel of pistols intended to be used with the shoulder stock. The regular rear sight was adjusted to allow for some upward rotation of the gun upon recoil, before the bullet left the muzzle. When a stock was attached, this movement was much reduced, and the center of pivot became the shoulder rather than the wrist. This changed the center of impact enough to require two different sight systems.

The biggest practical difference between the Dragoon and the Walker was that the Dragoon's short cylinder took 40 rather than 50 grains of powder, reducing its power by 20 percent. (It was also a little lighter, running 65 to 68 ounces, but it was still so big and heavy that this was hardly noticeable.) The full charge of the Walker was just too much. A number of test guns blew up and Colt didn't want to acquire a reputation for feeble machinery. A top strap joining the barrel to the top of the standing breech would have been a better solution, but Colt unaccountably resisted this improvement.

At that the Dragoon was no weakling. Forty grains of black powder is still a big charge, and spat that 219-grain bullet to over 900 f/s. This performance is quite similar to the current standard load for the .45 acp or the .44-40. The latter cartridge designator, in fact, means a .44 caliber bullet propelled by 40 grains of black powder—exactly what the Dragoon used.

The Walker and Dragoon Colts were unique in the history of fighting handguns, in that they were used at a time

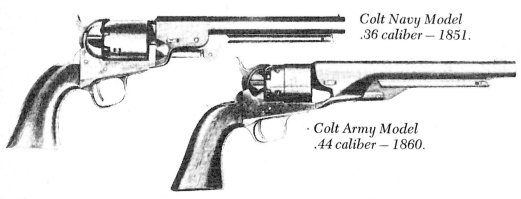

Colt Navy Model
.36 caliber — 1851.

· Colt Army Model
.44 caliber — 1860.

when long guns had not kept pace with advances in science, and for a while the pistol was actually superior to any two-hand gun that could be fielded.

The famed accuracy of the Kentucky rifle was countered by its fragility, low power, and most of all its deadly slowness in sustained fire. The regulation musket was powerful enough, and rugged, but it was still too slow on the second shot and it was hopelessly inaccurate. But the Colt revolver was rifled, unlike the musket, and compact, unlike the Kentucky, and capable of rapid fire, unlike either of them. It was a powerful man-stopper, and held in two hands it could stay on a man at 100 yards. A cavalry trooper, armed with one Dragoon on his belt, another on his saddle, and a shoulder stock to fit either in his pack, had only pity for the infantryman and his smoothbore musket!

Even during the Civil War, an officer armed with two Colts was the equal of 12 ordinary foot soldiers in a fight. The smoothbore musket died hard, and generations of perceptive infantry privates must have wondered why they were sent out to die with tools which couldn't measure up to competition. The answer was, I suppose, economy.

More progress came in 1851. The Dragoon was very cumbersome, in no sense a handy or convenient arm, and while the little pocket pistols of .31 caliber were no answer, there was room for compromise. Current metals did not permit a light gun of .44 caliber, but .36 was a possibility. This bore size was determined by the construction of a conical bullet which had the same shape as that of the conical .44 projectile, but the same weight as the round ball. Thus the .36 conical bullet weighed 140 grains, and when pushed by some 18 grains of black powder it was very similar to today's .38 Special. (Bore size was the same, since the .38 Special measures .357" across the grooves.) A round ball of .36 caliber weighs about 80 grains, and probably left the muzzle at a good rate of knots.

Several oldtimers who actually used it claimed it delivered better on men than the 140-grain conical slug. However, a British test held in 1852 established that the latter did pretty well, too, with better penetration at 100 yards than the issue musket.

Colt's effort in this direction was the 1851 Navy pistol. Through the tradition that it is easier to kill a sailor than a soldier, Colt was able to promote this new gun, which had proportions very similar to those of a modern heavy-duty revolver, as a service sidearm for the U.S. Navy, and it was so used from 1851 until the introduction of the Peacemaker in 1872.

The 1851 Navy .36 was very much lighter than the Dragoon, weighing only 38 ounces in its first versions. It couldn't match the Dragoon in power, but it quickly established a reputation as an easy and accurate gun to shoot. Its fine balance, light weight, and mild behavior made it very popular with those who felt the four-pound army pistol was just too much gun. The 1851 Navy was especially popular in California during the Gold Rush, and a number of famous duels were fought with it.

This gun was very popular in the Confederacy during the Civil War, and frequently mentioned as the regular sidearm of Southern officers. The true Colts had octagonal barrels while the Confederate copies were mostly round, otherwise it's often hard to tell which is which. The gun was 13 inches long with a 7½ inch barrel, and like all heavy-duty Colts since the Walker, it carried six shots. As is the case with all Colts which were in production for any considerable period, it appears with countless minor variations.

Colt went abroad in the '50s, and promoted his guns very widely. He set up shop in England and manufactured the Navy .36 there as well as some .31 pocket pistols. He visited Russia and Turkey, and did not neglect any of the belligerents in the Crimean War as markets for

13

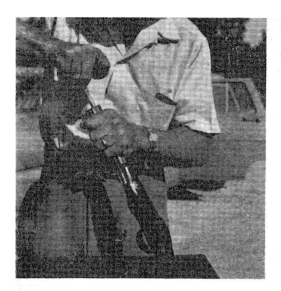

Loading a muzzle loader is slow . . .

acclaimed as all sorts of things, from the first semiauto to the ultimate "revolver" (though nothing about it revolved), but actually it was just a gadget, of technical interest only.

Just as Colt first saw the possibilities of joining the revolving breech to the percussion cap, Rollin White (inventor of the White sewing machine and the White steam car) saw the application of the self-contained cartridge to the revolver. He patented the idea of boring a cylinder clear through and loading it from the breech-end with metallic cartridges in 1855. He took his idea at once, of course, to Sam Colt. Colt was by this time far more of an industrialist than a gunman. Like so many examples of the type today, he was more interested in selling his products than improving them, even though his monopoly was due to expire in a year. He rejected White's system as unsafe and impractical, and thus opened the handgun business to a firm which has crowded the Colt name ever since. The firm was Smith and Wesson.

Horace Smith and Daniel Wesson had unsuccessfully challenged Colt's airtight patents in 1851, and had decided that while they waited for expiration in 1856, they would develop a new type of revolver which would not only equal but surpass the Colt. (In this they had more vision than Remington, who simply copied the Colt when the patent ran out, except for the solid frame improvement.) The advantage they sought in their new weapon was real utilization of the speed of reloading which the self-contained cartridge made possible. Their solution was the top-break, tip-up system. They bought White's patent, which extended to 1869, and brought out their "first model" revolver, a single action .22, in 1857.

The earliest rim-fire cartridges were foolishly feeble loads to fight with, and while the first S & W was an ingenious and beautifully finished arm, nobody in his right mind would take one into battle when he could get a .44 Colt or Remington. But there was all sorts of room for improvement, and while the Civil War

Guns of Old West

and the Reconstruction were carried on with cap-and-ball revolvers, Smith & Wesson were hot on the trail of a really effective cartridge pistol.

The top-break system is not strong enough for serious loads, and as long as they stuck to it, S & W were handicapped. They eventually worked up to some fairly hot rounds, but never one to match the .45 Colt cartridge of the 1873 Peacemaker.

A .32 rim-fire revolver was added in 1861, but this was like going to a tablespoon in place of a teaspoon for bailing out the boat, when what is needed is a bilge pump.

By 1864 Smith & Wesson had a real gun in experimental form, which was to develop into a very famous arm, but the confused commercial situation of the country at the time held up its production—while months rolled by and White's patent inexorably ran out.

There also was probably an element of complacency involved as well, for just as Colt had blocked competition in the previous 25 years, only S & W could sell you a breech loading revolver from 1856 to 1869. During this period the shooter could have a quick-loading pistol *or* a powerful pistol, but not both. Apparently enough customers would take rapidity and convenience of loading at any cost, so Smith & Wesson didn't have to worry.

Remington marketed some .44 rim-fire items in this period, by means of some interesting back door patent juggling, but not to the extent required to capture a large market.

During the immediate postwar period, Colt brought out the "Thuer Conversion," which could make any heavy-duty Colt since the Walker into a sort of semi breech loader. White's patent prevented boring Colt cylinders clear through (commercially), and the Thuer system used self-contained cartridges inserted from the front of the cylinder and fired by a pin which reached through a port in the rear which was actuated by the hammer. This device permitted optional use of a cap and ball cylinder, which was a strong point at a time when powder, lead and caps could be had at the most remote trading camp, but the new-fangled cartridges were obtainable only at well-stocked centers of population.

The Colt people also played down the breech loaders as both feeble and unsafe, as long as they couldn't manufacture any, but it's amusing to see how quickly they started making them as soon as they legally could. In fairness,

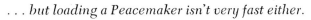

. . . but loading a Peacemaker isn't very fast either.

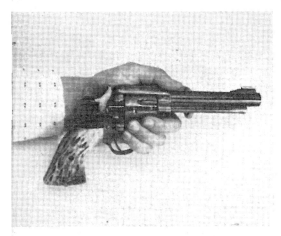

it should be noted that the Colt breech loader, when it appeared, was notably more powerful and of stronger construction than its competition.

In '69, the year their monopoly of repeating breech loaders ended, Smith & Wesson got their new gun on the market. It was known as the Single Action American and it took a .44 caliber, center-fire cartridge. Tyler Henry, inventor of the Henry repeating rifle which sired the famous Winchester lever guns, was the first man to see the possibility of large-caliber self-contained cartridges.

pistol. As the gun is opened all six empties are automatically flipped out. making loading a little quicker than is possible with today's "swing-out" revolver, which must be ejected manually.

At least 1000 "Americans" were furnished to the Army in '71, and Bill Cody got hold of one with which to impress the Grand Duke Alexis of Russia on their hunting trip in '69. When His Highness placed his order for 250,000 revolvers with Smith & Wesson, the company's competitive drive was numbed for a full five years. It's nice to have all your finan-

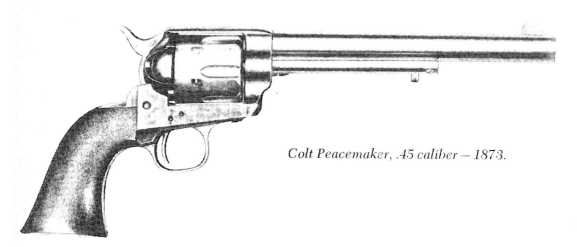

Colt Peacemaker, .45 caliber — 1873.

He expanded Houiller's .22's into the .44 Henry rim-fire, and pilot models of the S & W American were made to take this round. There was also an experimental .46 short rim-fire, pushing a 230-grain bullet with 26 grains of black powder — the heaviest rim-fire load ever made for handguns. But the "American" in commercial form took a center-fire round, a special cartridge taking a .43", 218 grain bullet and 25 grains of fuel. It wasn't up to the cap-and-ball load, but it *was* of sufficient power to be taken seriously.

The American featured the King system of simultaneous ejection, giving it the fastest reloading system available until the invention of the autoloading

cial problems solved, but everybody then goes out for coffee instead of tending the store.

The pistol made for the Russians was a lot like the American model. However, it had a 6½" barrel instead of 8", a different grip, it was somewhat lighter, and it took a different, Russian-designed cartridge. The .44 Russian is still with us today and makes a nice sub load for .44 plinking and practice. Its .432" diameter bullet weighs 246 grains and is pushed along at 750 f/s by 23 grains of black powder. It has always been a super-accurate round, and was a favorite on target ranges for decades. Nearly all the S & W Russians actually went to Russia, and many were still in use in both World Wars.

Smith & Wesson made some changes in their heavy pistol when they came down to earth again in 1875 after their honeymoon with the Czar. Finding the Peacemaker in full cry and the Army sold on .45 caliber, they produced the S & W "Schofield," featuring a much heavier barrel latch and taking a special .45 caliber cartridge. They couldn't make it to take the .45 Colt cartridge of the Peacemaker because of the essential weakness of the top-break system, but the .45 S & W round took the same 28-grain powder charge that the army arsenals loaded into the Colt cartridge. The full charge for the latter was 40 grains, but the army didn't feel it was necessary. Thus while the civilian Colt was a good deal more muscular than the S & W, in government use they were the same. You could use .45 S & W ammunition in a .45 Colt, but not vice versa. Some 6000 "Schofields" were made, and their adequate power and rapid loading made them very popular on the Frontier. Jesse James was partial to this gun, and was wearing one when he surrendered. Some say that Custer used one in his last fight, but after the Sioux left it was hard to tell for sure.

The S & W #3 "New Model" was introduced in 1878, going back to the gilt-edge .44 Russian round, and the weaker, pre-Schofield barrel latch. In fact, the #3 is in all basic respects a U.S. version of the Russian pistol. About 40,000 were sold, mainly as target and sporting weapons, up until 1905.

However, the most significant development of the period was Colt's re-entry into the handgun business. The company had not stopped operating, of course, but Sam Colt's death in '62, followed by that of Elisha Root, his chief technician and successor, in '65, had combined with S & W's control of the self-contained cartridge principle to dim the renown of the Colt name for some ten years. Old timers wondered whether the Colt tradition could be kept alive when Colt himself was no longer present to sustain it, but they also felt that if the company *did* decide to produce a breech loader it would be a good one. They were right, for the new gun was the Peacemaker.

It was officially called the "New Model Army Metallic Cartridge Revolving Pistol," later shortened to the "Single Action Army Pistol," on the popular advent of double action arms. It was patented in 1871 and marketed in 1873, when the first 200 were sold. It combined strength, reliability, simplicity, durability, medium weight, handiness, balance and power in a way that made it the most famous fighting handgun ever built.

The design of the Peacemaker is not attributable to any one person. The action and grip design are basically those of the original Walkers and thus came from Sam Colt himself. The top strap was finally borrowed from Remington "over Colt's dead body." The hammer was a modified form of that used on the 1860 Army—but the modification is an important improvement, and no one knows whose idea it was. Also, the rear sight was finally taken off the hammer and cut in the solid top strap. The cartridge was clearly an attempt to secure full Dragoon ballistics in a self-contained round—an excellent idea but certainly not a remarkable one, for everybody knew that a Dragoon could be relied on to lay a man out with one shot, while there was some doubt about lesser guns. The original loading of the Peacemaker cartridge (officially just ".45 Colt") was 235 grains of bullet and 40 grains of black powder. Later bullets weighed 250, 255, and 265, while powder charges dropped to 28 (U.S. Army) and rose to 45 (Remington commercial). Its modern standard load of smokeless powder is a sort of middle-sized version, starting a 250 or 255 grain bullet at 870 f/s in a 5½ inch barrel. Colt evidently went to .45 caliber, rather than the hitherto standard .44, to prevent the use of the new cartridge in 1860 pistols with altered cylinder. Since the actual diameter of a .44 is .432″ and that of the .45 Colt is .455″ the difference in bore size is greater than the designators indicate, and it is impossible to insert a loaded .45 Colt cartridge into a chamber bored for any .44 cartridge, current or obsolete.

However, the striking thing about the Peacemaker is its wonderful balance — the balance that made possible the art of the gunslinger. It snuggles into your hand in a way that is sensually comforting. Its weight rides just far enough forward to let you feel where it's pointing. With almost any hand it tends to line up the bore with the bones of the forearm, so that it shoots where you point it, without sights. And possibly best of all, it rolls out of a holster and lines up almost by itself, requiring less effort on the shooter's part than anything before or since.

I'm going to commit heresy and say that the marvelous balance of the Peacemaker is just a happy accident. If it weren't, the gun would never have been offered with its 7½-inch "cavalry-length" barrel. The long barrel makes the gun handle like an 1860 Army, and kills it for speed work. If, as is reported, Wyatt Earp claimed that the grotesque "Buntline Special," with its foot-long barrel, did not hinder his pistol work, it is simply evidence that Earp, a careful man, made very sure his gun was out and cocked before any trouble started!

I have always favored the 5½″ "artillery length" barrel for best balance, but the 4¾″ "civilian" barrel is highly regarded, and is possibly a shade quicker in clearing leather. Some velocity is lost as a pistol barrel is shortened, and in theory a longer distance between sights makes for more precise sighting, but I doubt if these matters are serious. I just like the feel of the 5½″ version and it's a nice compromise.

The Peacemaker is light for a serious sidearm, running 37 ounces in .45 Colt with the 5½″ barrel. With full Dragoon loads it kicked — not enough to trouble us in these days of 35-ounce .357's and 14-ounce .38 Specials, but enough to bother the army of the 1870's. This is evidently the reason why the army started loading it with only 28 grains of powder, seriously impairing its efficiency, especially against cavalry. I have not shot the old black-powder, full-charge load, but I can shoot the modern smokeless load in my Peacemaker with just the thumb and two fingers. The black powder load had only 40 f/s more and five grains less bullet — it couldn't have been too hard to manage.

Almost as soon as the Peacemaker appeared in .45 Colt, it was also offered in .44-40 as a companion piece to the Winchester Model 1873 rifle, to permit a man to equip himself with the same ammunition for both his long and short guns. It startles us today to think that anyone would feel adequately armed with a rifle using pistol ammunition, but Americans had got along for quite a while using the pipsqueak Kentucky rifles, and established a tradition of undergunning that is still with us today. Incidentally, the Peacemaker in .44-40 was called the "Frontier Model." In both sizes it sold for just $20.

The Peacemaker was soon being offered in every caliber under the sun, though the burly .45 Colt has always remained its most popular load. Some of the cartridges it was made for include .22 rim-fire, .32 Colt center-fire, .32 S&W center-fire, .38 (shorts and Special), .41 long and short Colt, .44 Colt, .44 Russian and Special, .45 Colt, .45 auto, and

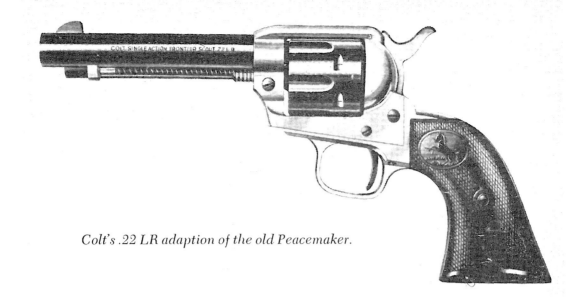

Colt's .22 LR adaption of the old Peacemaker.

.357. And in addition, if you had a rifle chambered for the .32-20, .38-40, or .44-40, or .44 Henry rim-fire you could get a Peacemaker made for the same round.

Remington went right along with Colt at this time, producing excellent sixguns in heavy calibers. They started in 1875 with the .44 Remington cartridge, which was almost the same as the .44-40, but quickly offered the same gun in .44-40 and .45 Colt. About the only thing the Remington offered over the Colt was a lanyard loop in the butt (a useful gadget if you have to sleep with your gun) but Remington never cut into the Peacemaker to any great extent. About 25,000 of the 1875 pistols were produced, and some 2000 of the improved 1890 version which was made in .44-40 only, but production stopped in 1894, leaving the field to Colt and Smith & Wesson.

Colt's 320,000 Peacemakers dominated the gunfighting era, but the company did produce a radically altered single action pistol in 1896, largely to compete with the #3 Smith & Wesson on the target range. This gun was known as the Bisley Model, and its main changes were intended to make a better target gun at the expense of its combat potential. Specifically, its grip was altered to place the axis of recoil lower in the hand, and its hammer was made easier to thumb on quick fire strings and less likely to disturb the aim when released. A target version of the Peacemaker was offered in 1888 as well, but these special models were never intended as real fighting handguns.

It's hard to discuss the Peacemaker without being carried away by the glamor of its illustrious past. This is the gun of Wyatt Earp and Bat Masterson. This gun roared in the saloons, on the boardwalks and along the cattle trails of the frontier. Custer's troopers went down in the sage brush above the Little Bighorn with these guns in their hands. When used by such wizards as Curly Bill Brocius and John Ringo, these guns were the instruments of an art not a bit less sophisticated than the aristocratic swordsmanship of the Renaissance. This gun permitted the deadly young Wes Hardin, before a roomful of witnesses, actually to "beat the drop"—the ultimate achievement in gunfighting. To do this you must draw and kill a man who is aiming a cocked gun at you, at short range,

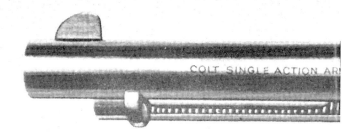

before he can react and squeeze a trigger. The Peacemaker did all this and more, for apart from the troopers, the peace officers and the professional gunmen, thousands of less renowned but equally hardy ranchers, prospectors, farmers, freighters and cowboys regarded the 1873 Colt as their one most important possession. A man could lose his money, his wagon, his clothes, or even his saddle, but he kept his sixgun.

Just to hold one in your hand produces a feeling of kinship with our western heritage—an appreciation of things like courage and honor and chivalry and the sanctity of a man's word.

Because of its record, we sometimes overrate the old gun. It was a wonderful tool in its day, but men designed it, and men have been able to make better guns since. The Peacemaker was undoubtedly the best fighting handgun of the Nineteenth Century, but it had a number of serious drawbacks, which have been remedied in today's sidearms.

First, in spite of what you may have heard, the Peacemaker was subject to breakage. Its action used flat springs throughout and they don't hold up like coils. Its cylinder lock spring was especially fragile—on my own gun it has broken twice. It is true that almost any part of the action could be repaired by the local blacksmith, but sometimes a blacksmith wasn't handy on the frontier.

Second, the Peacemaker wasn't too safe a gun, compared to today's weapons. Its hammer, when down, rests with its pin on the primer of the cartridge in line with the barrel. Strike it a sharp blow and it will fire. It is possible to lower the hammer between the rims of two rounds, but the cylinder cannot lock in this position and can be rotated accidentally into battery. There is a half-cock notch, for loading purposes, but it need wear only a bit before you can fire it from half-cock by a strong pull on the trigger, since the half-cock position is far enough back so that dropping the hammer from it will pop the primer. For these reasons most old timers carried the gun with the top chamber empty, only loading six rounds into their six shooters when they were certain things were about to smoke.

Lastly, the Peacemaker was murderously slow to load. The gun had to be brought to half-cock, the loading gate opened, and then each chamber had to be ejected and reloaded in turn, while the cylinder was rotated ⅙-turn by hand between each operation. This procedure wasn't much slower than reloading a cap-and-ball revolver, and it took the gun out of the fight. It was this that produced the two-gun man. He didn't use both at once, he carried a spare so he wouldn't be caught in action with an empty gun.

In 1957 Colt resumed production of its Single Action Army, the authentic Peacemaker, in 5½" and 7½" barrels only, and in two rather pointless calibers, .38 Special and .45 Colt. Any modern .38 Special, except the flyweight models, should be bored to take the .357 load if necessary. And the .45 Colt, while a grand old black powder cartridge, has been completely superseded by the .44,

Colt's modern single action Army — the Peacemaker.

which can use Russian or Special loads for practice and the mighty Magnum for business. The Colt produced today has none of the design improvements we might have wished, being identical, except for metallurgy and front sight width, with the Nineteenth Century pistol which sold for $20. And it sells for $125, over 500% more!

Today the Peacemaker, whether made by Colt, Ruger, or Great Western, must be regarded as a purely sporting arm. Its single action and impossible loading system rule it out of competition with modern double-action revolvers or auto pistols, where fighting is concerned. But happily it can still afford companionship, glamor and efficiency as a trail gun for outdoorsmen, and it's the odds-on favorite of quick draw fanciers. In .22 caliber, particularly in the 23-ounce, alumi-

num Ruger, and the new Colt "Frontier Scout," it's just right as a tin can gun for the youngsters. And in .357, or especially .44 Magnum, it's wonderful as a sidearm for backpackers, prospectors, fishermen, or other outdoorsmen who need a flat-shooting, powerful "substitute rifle" for camp meat, or conceivably camp defense. Naturally, accurate adjustable sights and a carefully tuned trigger are necessary for this sort of thing.

Finally, single action is always a safety feature for horsemen. The fact that you can't pull the trigger a second time and get a shot off, unless you deliberately cock the piece, can save much grief if your horse turns out to be unexpectedly gunshy. And if you just happen to fly out of the saddle, gun in hand, while coursing a coyote, it's nice to know you can't shoot yourself on landing.

Fast draw is important, but shooting straight is more so. Thrust gun straight forward from the right hip bone, and point entire forearm at the target.

Frontier Life Insurance

THE handgun occupies a special place in our western tradition, because circumstances combined to give it more importance in our pioneer society than an individual weapon usually rates. It was coincidental that the great surge of our westward movement occurred at a time when the design of short firearms had taken such huge strides that the pistol was actually a more efficient weapon in most ways than the rifle or musket. Not until the popular introduction of smokeless powder cartridges suitable for magazine rifles did the modern rifle-pistol relationship crystallize. And this took place just at the zenith of the revolver's utility.

So for a considerable period the pistol was actually the most useful fighting arm, and deferred to a two hand gun only where elephant-stopping power or ultra-long-range deliberate fire were required. During this period the pistol was a weapon of both defense and offense, which it is not today.

However, with the end of the Civil War and the beginning of the actual opening of the West, the real purpose of the handgun began to be understood—a purpose of vital importance which can never be fulfilled by a long gun of any sort.

The fighting pistol, in this new concept, was not the weapon of an aggressor. It was not the arm of anyone whose foremost concern was battle. On the contrary, it was the safeguard of a person trying his best to carry out his peaceful business of ranching, surveying, mining, running a store, or otherwise making a

living, but under circumstances where he might find a fight served up at any moment, without warning. This is the real mission of the sidearm, and while it was particularly applicable to the life of the pioneer, it remains identical and equally important today.

To fulfill such a mission, an efficient handgun must possess certain very definite characteristics, as follows:

a.) It must be dependable. There must never be any question about its doing what is expected of it, no matter what the circumstances.

b.) It must be *powerful. One* solid hit in the body must put a man out of action, *instantly* and *every time.*

c.) It must be handy. It must be worn constantly on the person in a way that permits instant access, so it cannot be so long or heavy or bulky that it becomes a nuisance.

d.) It must be capable of rapid controlled fire. Human enemies often run in packs.

e.) It must be manageable. Complicated operation, clumsiness, bad pointing characteristics, or uncontrollable recoil render it useless.

Very few sidearms in history meet these standards absolutely and without fail, but a number are from 85% to 95% effective. The others, except for target and sporting purposes, have no real value.

As we have seen, the 1851 Navy and 1860 Army Colts were good enough to approach true efficiency, but the Peacemaker was the instrument which showed the way and set the standard.

Because of its balance and the shape of its hammer, a Peacemaker can be slipped out of a properly designed holster, cocked and fired, with fair short range accuracy, in an incredibly short time. A man who took the trouble to master this technique was just about as dangerous with his gun in its everyday traveling condition as he was with it out and cocked. This odd fact made a tremendous impression on the culture of the

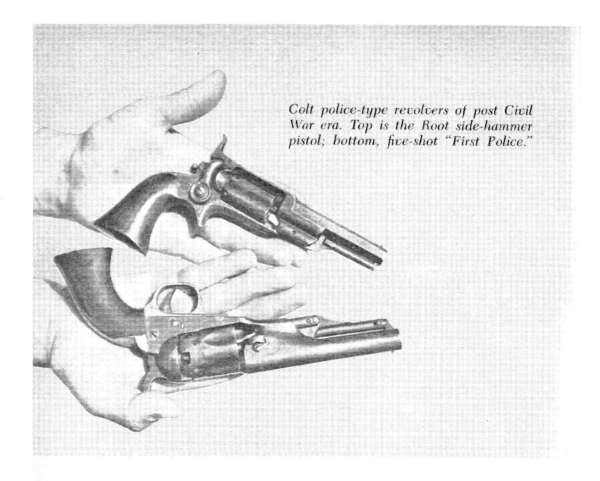

Colt police-type revolvers of post Civil War era. Top is the Root side-hammer pistol; bottom, five-shot "First Police."

period, fashioning a set of standards and a code of behavior which, in a somewhat exaggerated form, are the mainstay of today's show business.

Before the Peacemaker, holsters were invariably fully enclosed, flap-covered types, intended to protect the weapon from the elements. (Such rigs have their purpose today as trail-gun carriers.) But as soon as the pistol became handy enough to use quickly, the flaps were cut off and other variations were devised to permit carrying the weapon in a fashion which was both secure and fast.

Low-powered, small-bore, pocket pistols have always existed alongside the big sidearms, but the speed holster did not appear until really powerful weapons became handy. This would indicate that while the little pistols were widely sold to the uninformed, they were never taken seriously by anyone who had any real knowledge of violence.

When the introduction of breech loading made firearms less vulnerable to exposure, the fighting holster developed into an essential part of the weapon, and its evolution continues today. The three requisites of comfort, security and speed are sometimes joined by the necessity for concealment to pose a problem which is not easy to solve. For instance, most of the western-type quick-draw holsters marketed today have no security at all. Just running upstairs with them, much less riding a horse, will lose your gun.

The old prints taken in the '80's suggest that the "full-house," buscadero gun belt and holster of today did not exist in the day of the gunfighter, but the open-top cutaway pouch holster was apparently worn on a rather loose waist belt to bring it lower to the hand. Gunfights were seldom carried out in the classic, middle-of-the-street style dear to the hearts of scriptwriters, and when your gun is slung way down your right thigh it may be handy when you're standing erect but very awkward when sitting at a poker table.

In any case, the thing which distinguished the gunfighter era from the previous age was the use of the gun "from the leather." The Peacemaker made this possible and the gunfighters designed their own leather.

In a wilderness there is little need for law, since men seldom meet and thus don't have much occasion for quarreling or referees. But as the country is invaded by new people, crowding brings conflict faster than the law can be brought in to handle it, and some sort of generally accepted code must suffice for justice until the land is tamed and the people with it.

During the pioneer days of the West a set of rules governed a man's conduct, independent of any formal law or any enforcing agency. Men who obeyed the

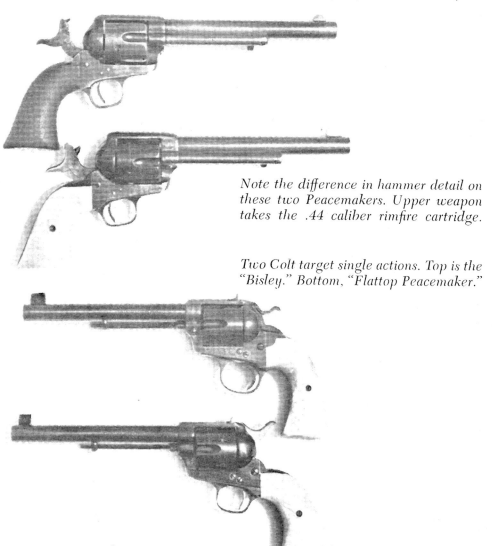

Note the difference in hammer detail on these two Peacemakers. Upper weapon takes the .44 caliber rimfire cartridge.

Two Colt target single actions. Top is the "Bisley." Bottom, "Flattop Peacemaker."

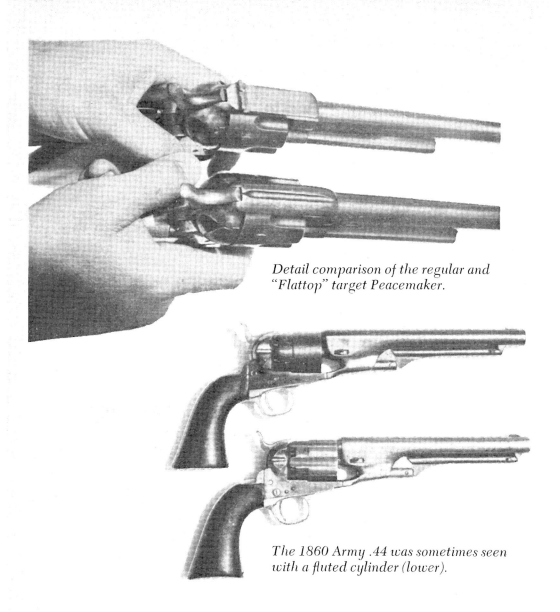

Detail comparison of the regular and "Flattop" target Peacemaker.

The 1860 Army .44 was sometimes seen with a fluted cylinder (lower).

rules could count on the respect and support of others. Men who broke them outlawed themselves and had no rights. We all know these rules today almost as well as those who lived by them. A man pays his gambling debts first. A man's word is kept, even if it kills him. A man may not accept an insult. A stranger must be fed. A man does not shoot another in the back or from ambush. Horse thieves hang. These are a few, but the one that concerns us here is this: a man may not be held accountable for the outcome of a fair fight. The implication is plain — if you're going to survive, either learn to win your fights or stand back out of the way. Likewise, fight decisively. A sore loser is no threat to you if he's dead. Fist-fighting was out of the question — it settled nothing and risked damage to your gun hand.

The heart of the matter was the definition of "fair." It varied from place to place, but in general if both parties were equally armed, aware of the situation, and started together, the loser had no social, moral or legal recourse. The man who made the first move had the burden of proof—if he lost, his surviving opponent not only was free of blame, but even acquired a measure of esteem.

As skill in the use of handguns grew, certain talented and hard-training experts got so good that no special arrangements were necessary to make certain of the outcome of a "fair" fight, as long as their adversary, or rather victim, was not a man of similar ability. Experiments made in modern times indicate that a totally untrained man takes between 1½ and 3 seconds to get off a controlled shot from the leather. An ordinary good shot takes about a second. An expert can make it in half that. So while the sharpie might provoke a duffer into a "fair fight,"

the result was morally murder. Between two experts, on the other hand, there was never any assurance as to the outcome. The difference between the world's best gunslinger and any other ace is so slight that the loser's bullet is on its way before the winner's shot can affect its aim.

Many interesting techniques arose out of the efforts of intelligent or ruthless men to live by the code and still minimize risk. After all a fight had only to *seem* fair to qualify. A skillful tactician could so plan a meeting that he had a decisive edge which was not apparent to spectators, or even to his foe. Conditions of light, range, background, and physical position could be planned in advance of a meeting to produce a situation which met all the requirements of a

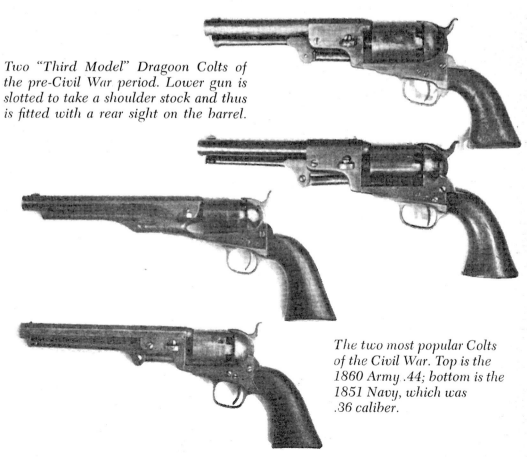

Two "Third Model" Dragoon Colts of the pre-Civil War period. Lower gun is slotted to take a shoulder stock and thus is fitted with a rear sight on the barrel.

The two most popular Colts of the Civil War. Top is the 1860 Army .44; bottom is the 1851 Navy, which was .36 caliber.

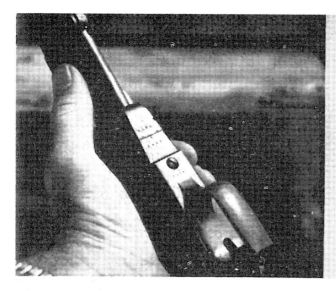

Walker No. 1010. Sam Walker had this gun in his hand when he was killed by a Mexican lancer (his gun was empty).

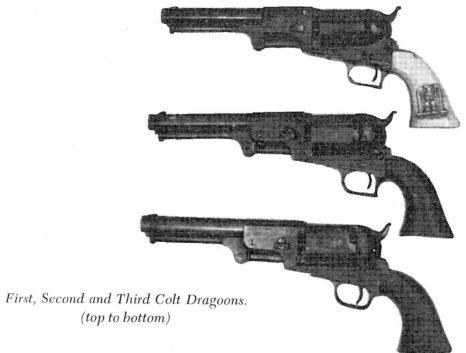

First, Second and Third Colt Dragoons.
(top to bottom)

"fair" fight, but which actually was a long way from it.

Gene Cunningham tells of a dude gambler who ran afoul of a well known hard case at the gaming tables. The latter informed him that he'd better leave town within the hour or pick out his plot in boot hill. The dude was no great hand with a gun but disliked the thought of running just because a professional tough told him to. The gunman left the scene with the promise that he would be back shortly to enforce his demand, and the gambler's friends advised him that he'd best clear out. But the matter was simpler than anyone expected. As the hour ran out the dude took up his position, back to the bar, facing the swinging doors, pistol in hand. The hard case came blustering in, but his gun was holstered. The gambler simply covered him, letting him try to beat the drop or back down.

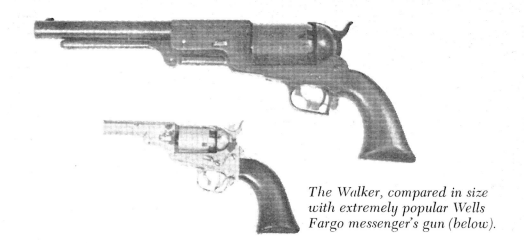

The Walker, compared in size with extremely popular Wells Fargo messenger's gun (below).

The gunman, fearing for his reputation, took the chance and, not surprisingly, lost. This was held to be a fair fight and the gambler went his way rejoicing.

One thing that should be cleared up, while we're on the subject, is the accuracy potential of the western gunslinger. Anyone who has ever tried it, from Bill Hickok's day to this, knows that maximum speed and button-hole accuracy don't go together. The accuracy necessary to hit a man in the body, at a range of 20 feet, is what is necessary to a gunfighter in a speed situation. If the range is any greater the problem becomes one of judging just how much of your maximum speed must be sacrificed in order to hit your target. No man from Wes Hardin to Delf Bryce can hit a man reliably at 25 yards, when using his fastest draw. It takes a highly trained pistol man to hit a silhouette 10 times out of 10 at 25 yards from the leather, given two full seconds from the signal to the shot. And there is no sense in saying that today's marksmen aren't what they were in Tombstone days—because they're better. They have better equipment, better training methods, much more ammunition, and exactly the same motivation — survival.

The western gunfighter was undoubtedly accurate enough for his purposes. The big .45 bullet could be relied on if

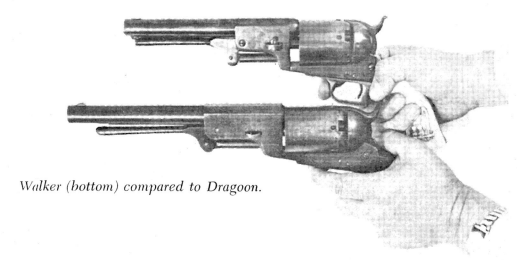

Walker (bottom) compared to Dragoon.

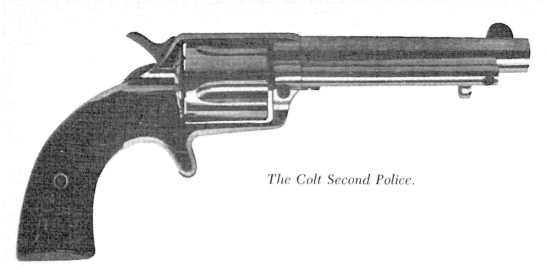

The Colt Second Police.

it struck anywhere in a man's trunk — a large target. But we hear a lot about sheer speed, as if the *fastest* draw was what made a gunfighter famous. Available records indicate that speed, like accuracy, was necessary up to a certain point, after which it became academic. The gunslinger had to work until he completely dominated an untrained or semi-trained antagonist. Beyond that only very small increases were possible, so small that for any practical purpose they don't count. To allow a foe to initiate action and then to hit him before he can get off a controlled round requires approximately double his speed. You *can* be twice as fast as a duffer, but you're never going to be twice as fast as

any really good man. And a 15% edge is no help to you — it won't save your life.

The oldtimers, lacking stopwatches, used the poker chip as their index of speed. To match yourself against them you place a silhouette target 20 feet in front of you, stand facing it with your gun in the leather, and extend your arm, shoulder high, toward the target with a poker chip on the back of your hand. Whenever you're ready, draw and hit that target in the breadbasket before that chip hits the ground. (Don't cheat by flipping the chip upward — just let it drop.) If you can do this every time, you can be sure that you have all the physical skill you need to have held your own in Dodge, Abilene, Tombstone, or El Paso

Remington Model 1871 Army single shot pistol.

Top, the Peacemaker; center, the Walker; bottom, the 1860 Army. All are .44 caliber. Note the practically identical grip design.

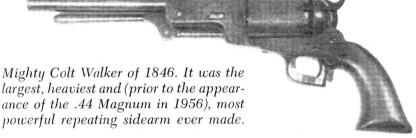

Mighty Colt Walker of 1846. It was the largest, heaviest and (prior to the appearance of the .44 Magnum in 1956), most powerful repeating sidearm ever made.

back in the days when you might have been called upon to prove it. What you probably *don't* have is the type of mind necessary to take advantage of your lethal skill.

Because mental attitude is what makes a deadly gunman, on either side of the law. This point is so important that it is the whole key to the sometimes inexplicable circumstances of gunfighting. Yet it is hardly ever mentioned, or even admitted, in our current fiction media. The fact is that while a certain level of both speed and accuracy must first be reached, from that point on a successful gunfighter must have a killer's mind.

In all but a few psyches there is a strong instinctive block against taking human life. Most people can kill if they must, but the decision to kill is reached only under very powerful stimulation, which takes time to build up. The decisive edge in a gunfight goes to the combatant who first discovers that he is in a killing situation. If he makes up his mind just ⅛th of a second before his opponent, he will win, providing both men are roughly similar in speed and the first shot doesn't miss. If a man makes up his mind to kill before a meeting, and his foe is not quite sure of this in his own mind, only an accident can save the latter.

If *both* parties have made the mortal

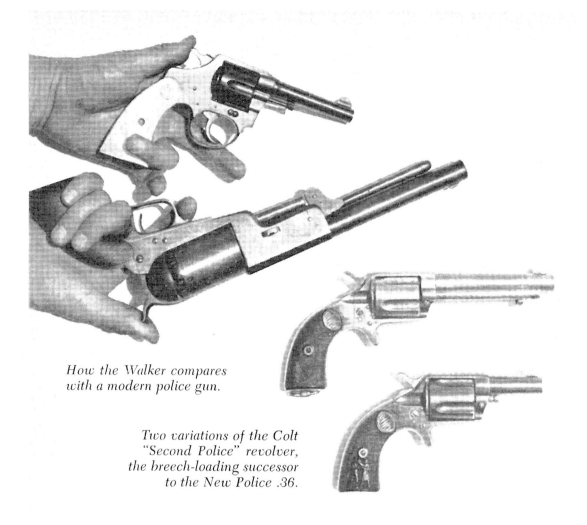

How the Walker compares with a modern police gun.

Two variations of the Colt "Second Police" revolver, the breech-loading successor to the New Police .36.

decision before they meet the result is not pistol-type gunfight, but more of a pitched battle which really should be settled with rifles. If only pistols are available, coolness and marksmanship win the round. The famous case in point is Hickok's killing of Dave Tutt in Springfield, Mo., in 1865. Both men *had* decided on killing, probably as much as 24 hours before the encounter. Contact was made diagonally across the town square, a matter of 75 yards—much too great a range for any speed work. But Tutt couldn't hold his nerve. He drew and sprayed rapidly in Hickok's general direction. With his cold, killer's poise Bill steadied his hold with two hands (possibly using a post rest) and pinwheeled Tutt with one round. Now there are plenty of qual-

ified pistolmen who can hit a man, from a steady position, at 75 yards, but few have the sort of reptilian self-control to select a rest and squeeze off a target-type shot when their adversary is kicking up dust and plucking at leaves in their immediate vicinity with .44 caliber talons. Tutt got off four shots before Hickok fired, clearly demonstrating the futility of "area" fire at 75 yards. (Have you ever wondered why these show business heroes advance up to quick draw range in the middle of the cowtown's main street? All that would be necessary would be a careful shot from prone way down by the corner saloon!)

I don't mean to suggest that a quick draw is not an essential matter to a man who lives by his gun, but that the ability

Long gun accuracy with a revolver might well be attained in this manner. Reports indicate that Bill Hickok may have used this method to kill Dave Tutt in a duel.

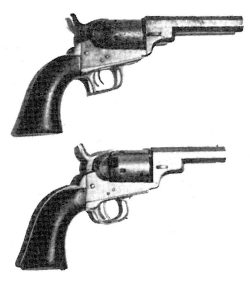

Two Colt pocket cap and ball revolvers of .31 caliber. Top one is "Baby Dragoon," bottom one is the "Wells Fargo."

to size up a situation instantly, decide that killing is indicated, and select the appropriate tactics with not the slightest hesitation about the taking of a life—this is far more important! The fastest man who ever lived would die with his gun in his holster, facing his killer helplessly, if he had no previous idea that a fight was forthcoming. A smooth, deliberate draw is completed in the time it takes for an unwarned man to think, "My God, he's going to shoot me!" and initiate his own response. Therefore a moderately fast man who is ready to kill without giving it a thought is a much deadlier gunfighter than a veritable magician with the handgun who is held back by normal scruples.

The oldtimers couldn't afford much consideration for the enemy and plenty of mishaps, in which the wrong man got it, were the result. To use Hickok again as an example, he was never one to wait for someone else to start. He killed his close friend, Mike Williams, when the latter ran up behind him during a tough situation.

And there is one other point about gunslinging efficiency that shouldn't be missed. In addition to owning a complete lack of concern about other men's lives, the deadliest sort of gunman cares not a damn about his own, either. The consensus of those who knew all the players in Tombstone's roaring saga points up two men above the rest as the ones most to be avoided in combat. John Ringo, the self-despising ruin of a cultured gentleman; and Doc Holliday, the blonde spectre of a dentist, dying of tuberculosis. Each had the killer's mind—and each had the extra quality of complete indifference to his own death. In fact, both Ringo and Holliday seem to have sought death at gunpoint in preference to the prospect of living on in a private hell. Facing a man like that, when you hold your own life dear, is comparable to a dice game in which you stake your entire fortune and the other man plays with match sticks. ∎

Double Action

IT is widely held that double-action was the next important step in sidearm development after the introduction of self-contained cartridges and breech-loading. It is certainly true that the double-action revolver is much the most popular business pistol in the U.S. today. But double-action was not common in the Old West, even though its technical principles had been worked out prior to the Civil War.

Strictly speaking a double-action revolver is one whose action operates in two ways, either by cocking the hammer with the thumb, and dropping it by a very short, almost imperceptible, motion of the trigger, or, by pulling the trigger through a long, continuous stroke which raises the hammer from full down to full cock positions and drops it, without any actuation other than the trigger itself. In revolvers this long stroke also unlocks, rotates and locks the cylinder.

The term has been corrupted with use

so that today we refer to the first method as single-action shooting and to the second as double-action, whether or not the weapon used is capable of either or both systems of operation. Likewise we refer to pistols which require thumb cocking as "single-action," those which can be cocked only by the long trigger stroke as "double-action only," and those which can be used either way as "selective double-action."

Colt's earliest competition, the Deane-Adams revolver of 1851, used the trigger-cocking principle and made much of its advantages in rapid fire. It was not strictly speaking a double-action gun since it could not be thumb-cocked, but we would call it so today. Colt quite rightly sneered at this so-called advantage since in gaining rapidity of fire it sacrificed accuracy, but any impartial gun bug could see that only a small change was necessary to provide both types of action in one system. It was

The Colt double action Army — 1877.

only a couple of years before Beaumont of England introduced true double-action, or selective double-action as it is now known, but it took more than two decades for it to be offered in America in a serious caliber, and almost another quarter century after that before it was really accepted by the public. Double-action pocket guns were experimented with all along, but they were mostly sold to people who had no real need for a weapon.

Double-action's backward childhood is explicable on several grounds. First, there was the inevitable distrust of what was held to be a more complicated and fragile mechanism. You will recall that this same sort of backwoods prejudice hampered Colt in '36, and was one of the reasons for the Paterson plant's failure. It crops up today in the revolver vs. auto-pistol arguments. Second, and more important, the pistolmen of the westward movement were very practical in their gunning, and they well knew that accuracy of fire is far more desirable than volume. It's much easier for any but the double-action specialist to hit with the crisp, single-action let-off, and a man hit with one round from a Peacemaker is much less dangerous than a man scared by a burst of double-action fire. Third, single-action revolvers, particularly the Peacemaker, could be shucked empty by "fanning" even faster than a double-

action gun, if there were ever a call for it. You couldn't hit anything this way, but if you wanted to hit something you cocked either gun. And fourth, the early double-actions were extremely stiff and hard to use, their single-action (thumb-cocked) trigger pulls were terrible, and they couldn't compare in balance to the Colt and Remington single-action guns.

However, both Colt and Smith & Wesson felt the market was there and brought out their first double-action revolvers in 1877.

The S & W was clearly designed as a back-up gun, a handy reserve weapon for concealed use where a full-bore side-arm might not be indicated. It was a five-shot break-top item taking a fat little .38 cartridge which will *not* fit into a .38 Special chamber. It flung a .359", 146-grain bullet with 14 grains of black powder, a somewhat less emphatic load than the cap and ball .36's, but about as much as one could expect from a "stingy-gun." The same round is loaded today with smokeless powder and similar ballistics. The Smith *was* popular, and it gave the company such confidence in the double-action principle that in 1887 an enclosed-hammer model was offered which could not be thumb-cocked at all —now known as a "double-action only" revolver. To my mind this was a step backward—limiting the gun's usefulness for no valid reason—but Smith & Wesson don't feel this way and today produce the "Centennial," the only "single-system-double-action" gun still made.

Weapons of Billy the Kid's last fight. Top is a .41 Lightning, as used by Billy. Bottom, a .45 Peacemaker like Pat Garrett's.

Smith & Wesson double action .38—1877.

Colt entered the field with both big and little guns. The "Lightning" in .38 and .41 caliber competed with the Smith & Wesson as a back-up gun. The .38 round was very similar to the Smith cartridge and ammunition could be interchanged. The .41 was a bit better, using a 200-grain bullet of true .38 caliber (the only pistol pellet I've been able to find that is really a .38. The .38 Specials and 9 mm's are actually .36″ while the .38-40 is actually .40″). The Lightning offered six shots to the S & W's five, and it used the very strong, solid frame design of the Peacemaker, but it was just as slow to load as its big brother, while the Smith could be cleared with a flick of the wrist.

W. H. Bonney, Billy-the-Kid, was one of the first well-known gunmen to take up double-action, and he used a pair of .41 Lightnings with dexterity. He was "had" by Pat Garrett's Peacemaker, and since Pat fired in the dark without sights, his gun's superb balance might be held responsible for the victory of law and order. Also, its brutally effective load paralysed Billy with one hit, so that, while he had his double-action Lightning in his hand and was very much "on the prod," he couldn't get off a single return shot. If Garrett had been using a .38 Special he might well have died with Billy.

Also in '77 Colt brought out the "Double-Action Army" revolver, a scaled-up version of the Lightning taking the standard .45 round of the Peacemaker. This was a big, brawny gun with a 7½″ barrel, solid-frame, rod-ejection, a bird's head grip, and a weight of 40 ozs. It was adopted by the army and about 60,000 were made, including a variation with an oversized trigger-guard for gauntleted use. It offered no advantage over a Peacemaker except the dubious one of double-action, while it was much clumsier and very awkward for speed work. It was discontinued in 1909.

It is interesting to note that Remington, as well as some others, built double-action cap and ball pistols during the Civil War which were practically identical with their current military models except for that feature. But Remington didn't think enough of the idea to incorporate it in their fine Peacemaker-type revolvers of the latter part of the century. Oddly, their double-action cap and ball .36 Navy was produced clear up until 1888.　■

Two Colt "Storekeepers," distinguished by absence of regular ejector system. Below, customary Peacemaker version, top is the very rare "double action" type.

When Colt went double action in 1877, the "Lightning" top was offered in .38 and .41 calibers; "double action Army" (bottom) took .45 Peacemaker cartridge.

The long Guns

THE "Kentucky" rifle will always stand out in the history of the United States. It was the aristocrat of the colonial and revolutionary periods, and it laid the foundations of the tradition of American marksmanship. Slow, low-powered, crudely sighted, clumsy, and fragile, it had one big thing in its favor—*accuracy*. In the hands of an expert, and at the short ranges imposed by the dense eastern forests, it literally could hit anything that could be seen, every time. It didn't hit very hard, but you don't have to hit a man in the eye very hard to kill him. Thus, for individual combat or hunting in thick cover, the Kentucky was truly great. For opening hostilities at 60 yards against musket-carrying regulars it was murderous, but after that first volley the party was over. On several bloody occa-

sions in the Revolution, the stolid British infantry gritted its teeth and faced that deadly blast, after which the survivors pushed in with the bayonet and "dispersed the rabble."

The Kentuckies (actually built mainly in Pennsylvania) were long, light, flintlock rifles. Their carefully made barrels had very slow rifling and averaged about .36 caliber. Their round lead bullets of some 80 grains weight were cast slightly under bore size and were hooked to the rifling by means of a "patch." This was a disk of greased linen or flannel which was centered over the muzzle after the powder was loaded, to receive the ball. It formed a snug bond between steel and lead, centered the ball in the barrel, acted as a gas check, and also tended to wipe excess powder fouling down onto

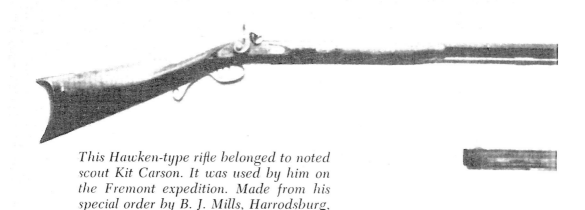

This Hawken-type rifle belonged to noted scout Kit Carson. It was used by him on the Fremont expedition. Made from his special order by B. J. Mills, Harrodsburg, Ky., in 1842, it measures 48⅜ inches.

the charge at each loading. It was a fine system for obtaining accuracy but took too much time and care for combat use. One shot was the rule for the buckskin boys—after that they generally used a tomahawk.

When the Louisiana Purchase opened the vast Mississippi-Missouri watershed to the Americans, they started out to explore it with Kentuckies, but found out at once that they were going to need something better. First, when the forest stopped and the prairie began, the range at which a rifle was used opened way out, and the light, round ball of the Kentucky lost velocity sadly beyond 60 yards. Second, the bison and the grizzly took a great deal more killing than the white-tailed deer and the inoffensive black bear. And third, the plains Indians were cavalrymen, sweeping to attack in flying swarms rather than slipping individually from tree to tree. More rapid fire became important.

The famed answer to this was the Hawken rifle and others of the same type by other makers. Heavy frontier rifles existed earlier, of course, for the British and Dutch had need of them in Africa, but while some of these found their way to the New World, they were far too costly to become popular with the mountain men. The Hawken, on the other

hand, was plainly finished, ruggedly built, made right in St. Louis, and sold for just $25.

Jake and Sam Hawken set up shop at the gateway to the fur country in 1822. They built their heavy, caplock, medium-length rifles as fast as they could up until the middle '60's, when breech-loading superseded them. The guns weighed 10½ to 12½ pounds and came in calibers from .44 to .53, with larger bores available on order up to .60". The .50 caliber Hawken was a popular size, firing a round ball of some 200 grains with an equal charge of black powder. As with the Kentucky, the twist of the rifling was quite slow, averaging 40", and the heavy octagonal barrels ran from 34" to 38" in length. (As any novice ballistician knows, the shorter the bullet the slower the twist necessary to stabilize it, and vice versa. A round ball is the easiest form of missile to stabilize, since it actually need not remain point-on at all.)

The features of great ruggedness, percussion ignition, low cost and adequate power made the Hawken a natural for the early plainsmen. Where Daniel Boone and Davy Crockett used Kentuckies, Jim Bridger and Kit Carson used Hawkens.

Accuracy was not generally up to that of the lighter gun, but it could be had

Famous Jim Bridger rifle, now owned by F. C. Clark, Los Angeles, Calif., in whose family it has been for many years. Bridger had this fine gun with him when he discovered Great Salt Lake and Yellowstone.

if you had time to use patches. If not, you still had fair prospects, since the larger bore permitted a slightly tighter ball to be loaded bare. Modern tests indicate that 12 inch groups at 200 yards were possible, and this is not bad at all. Also, you didn't have to hit your man in the eye—that big, heavy slug struck a serious blow.

Claims of the period indicate a rate of fire of five rounds per minute—12 seconds per load—and an effective range of 350 yards. Just what is meant by "effective" is a question, but as most Hawkens were fitted with set triggers, it's evident that precision work with them was considered distinctly feasible.

No one gun "Won the West," but the gun that explored it from the Mississippi to the Pacific was the Hawken.

MINIE HAD A BALL

The problem of slow loading in a "front feeding" rifle seemed insurmountable for a long time. Accurate range and rapid sustained fire just didn't go together, and most of the world's armies simply gave up and issued smooth-bore muskets to their men, along with instructions to get up close before firing. That "whites-of-their-eyes" line was dead serious. But it takes tragically magnificent discipline to advance directly up to musket range while your scatheless enemy calmly erases your leaders and front ranks with rifles. Such discipline can be had, but it's rare. And, as it turned out, unnecessary.

With the musket you just rolled your round ball down the muzzle, or thrust it quickly home with a ramrod as fouling built up. With a rifle you had to patch your ball with great care, or drive a tightly-fitted bullet home against the rifling with a mallet. Speed *or* accuracy, but not both, was the word.

The solution to this matter came from Colonel Minié of the French Army, and became known as the Minié ball. Actually it is no ball at all, but a cylindrical bullet, semi-pointed at the front end and having a conically hollow base. Its principle is simple. The bullet is cast sufficiently under bore size to permit it to slip down the barrel without engaging the rifling. On firing, the powder charge upsets the base, forcing it out, umbrella-fashion, against the rifling. This works, and it arrived just in time for the main event. For while we fought the Revolution with muskets and Kentuckies, and 1812 (mainly New Orleans) with Kentuckies, and opened the West with Hawkens, and fought the Mexican War

Sharps rifle owned by Bill Tilghman, famous lawman and gunfighter. With this gun, Tilghman killed an estimated 7500 buffalo. Note rawhide strip binding the split stock.

with flintlock muskets and such Colt pistols as could be had, we fought the Civil War with Minié rifles.

They were made in all sizes and shapes, and in calibers ranging from .58 to .71. The most common sizes were .58 and .69. It was customary to supply each bullet with a standard charge of powder attached to it in a varnished paper cylinder, making up a self-contained cartridge which could be rammed home with one stroke. When this was combined with the Maynard tape primer (invented in 1845 by a D.C. dentist and strikingly similar to the cap roll of a repeating cap pistol) it made possible a three-second load, only fractionally slower than that of a breech-loading single-shot. Of course you still had to stand erect to load that fast, so it was not really up to breech-loading, but it was a tremendous step forward.

Ballistics of the Minié rifles and carbines varied radically with bore size, bullet configuration, and particularly with powder granulation. To seat properly into the rifling, the "skirt" of the bullet must be upset uniformly and almost instantly, and this requires relatively fine granulation. But too fine a grain produces dangerously steep pressure curves, and since most of the rifles had strip welded iron barrels, they couldn't take that sort of thing. So a middle ground was sought between loose bullet fit and a burst gun. Even when the best balance is obtained, modern tests indicate that about one shot in 20 will be a flyer, due to failure to upset.

Minié's were extremely powerful when a good compromise was reached. The .69 bullet weighed 700 grains and departed at between 800 and 1000 f/s. 70 grains of ffg powder was standard for

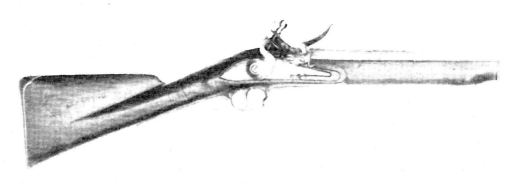

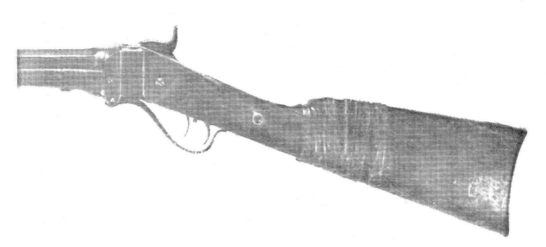

.69 caliber, and 60 for the .58's. 90 grains is about maximum for these guns, but again velocity is affected more by granulation than by the weight of the charge. It's possible to throw a lot of unburned powder with a 90-grain load if it's too coarse, and to blow up the gun with 60 grains if it's too fine.

In the field the Minié rifles worked very well, considering the standards of training, discipline and marksmanship common to the citizen armies involved. Fifty to one hundred rounds could be fired between cleanings, against about 10 for a round ball rifle, allowing them to remain in action throughout all but the heaviest engagements without a breathing spell. Discounting the five percent of flyers, groups of eight to twelve inches at 100 yards were possible—about the equal of a Dragoon Colt in the hands of a very good shot. Such standards may

not impress the minute-of-the-angle league, but they are about as high as one can expect from people basically uninterested in shooting, using open sights. After all, such a distinguished authority as Townsend Whelen holds that 200 yards is the effective limit of iron sights, and these rifles would usually stay on a man's torso at that range.

There *were* good riflemen in the Civil War, and both snipers and optical sights appeared. Usually, however, they did not use Minié rifles, but stuck to weapons of the Hawken type using a patched ball. Two regiments of marksmen were organized on the Union side, known as "Berdan's Sharpshooters," and equipped with Colt revolving rifles and scope sights. The Colt principle avoided the problems of rifling engagement since the bullet did not have to traverse the barrel before firing and thus could be a tight fit with-

British Brown Bess flintlock in .75 caliber.

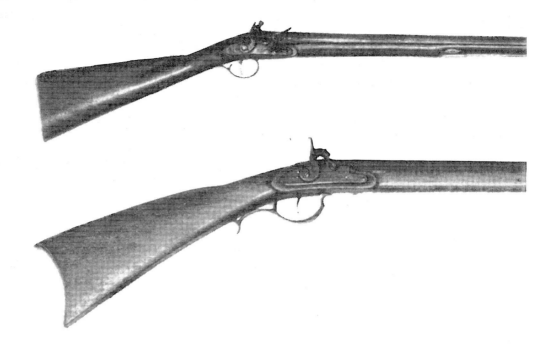

MINIE BALL

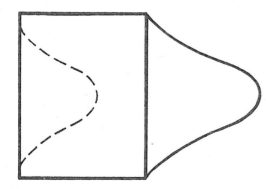

out slowness. Reports suggest that the Colts were about midway in accuracy between a patched Hawken and a good Minié rifle, and of course they were six-shooters besides.

Today the Minié ball survives in our pneumatic gallery guns, whose "skirted" pellets use exactly the same principle as those of the rifles with which we fought our greatest war.

RAPID FIRE

Repeating fire, more or less continuous, was an obvious goal of ordnance design from the very beginning of firearms.

New England flintlock Kentucky with 50½" barrel.

This smoothbore is a .50 caliber weapon. The 37½ inch barrel is half-round, half-octagonal.

It is of no value to the sportsman, but it can be absolutely vital to anyone involved in combat, whether defending his home and family, maintaining law and order, or fighting a war. Volume fire, always and essentially combined with accuracy, can make one man the equal of many, and has made possible feats of valor which, for better or for worse, have changed history.

True rapid fire was not possible prior to the appearance of "self-exploding-metallic cartridges," but Sam Colt came up with a good stop-gap, and his long guns were the forerunners of the breed of repeating rifles which figured so

largely in our post-Civil War chronicles.

The Paterson factory produced two models of revolving rifles—the 1837 and 1839. The former was a "hammerless" model with a cocking ring forward of the trigger guard, while the latter used the conventional central hammer to cock, rotate and lock the cylinder. These guns were made in various calibers and with chambers holding from five to eight rounds. They were weak in that they followed the open frame design of the pistols, and this was strong enough neither for the support of a full barrel nor for the sort of charge which was expected in a rifle. However, they were tested at a

This U.S. Winchester model '73 rifle is a 17-shot, .44-40 weapon. Barrel measures 30 inches.

practical rate of 60 aimed shots in 10 minutes, and this was unprecedented. We have seen that a Hawken muzzle loader could deliver possibly 50 rounds in the same period, providing its operator didn't wear out his hands, but the significant difference was that the Colt, once loaded, provided several shots in *immediate* succession, enough to dispose of most minor affrays which might arise. This proved quite sensational at the time, especially in Florida where the Seminole campaigns were in progress, and Sam Colt pushed his rifles and carbines there perhaps more vigorously even than his pistols, as shown by the fact that Uncle Sugar actually bought small numbers of them just before the Paterson plant folded.

When Colt finally got rolling at Hartford, he tried again on the rifle angle, but this time he avoided the open frame weakness. The Hartford rifles used a frame similar to that of the 1855 pocket pistols, which is solid over the cylinder, and also used the Root "sidehammer" of the little guns. These rifles were made in .36, .40, .44, and .50 caliber with a six-shot cylinder; and in .56 caliber with five shots. The barrels varied from 24 to 31 inches in length, and appeared both octagonal and round, with or without a fore-end. They seem to have been good guns, and were highly commended in contemporary writings. Good sights were available at extra cost, and a scope was actually a catalog factory option. We haven't caught up with that to this day!

Two disadvantages were mentioned about Colt's long guns. First, the gap between cylinder and barrel produced a blast which was too close to the face for the average trooper's peace of mind, and consequently only experienced shots enjoyed shooting these guns. Second, they cost too much. Forty dollars in 1860 was a large figure. By comparison (since a standard service Colt revolver cost $17.69 then and $140 now) the rifle went for the equivalent of $308.

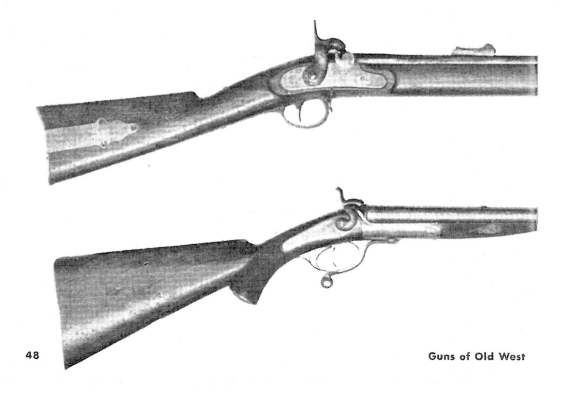

Be that as it may, some 7000 long Colts were built during the Civil War, and quite a few were carried in it as officers' personal weapons.

The War saw all sorts of breech-loading experiments, mainly applied to cavalry carbines, but there was one honest-to-Christofer repeater available at the outset, albeit untried and in very limited numbers. This was the Henry, produced by O. F. Winchester at the New Haven Arms Company. The Henry, named for the pioneer cartridge inventor Tyler Henry, was a lever-action, tube-magazine, repeating rifle taking a .44-caliber rim-fire pistol cartridge, and it was produced in 1860. Its 200-grain bullet was propelled by 28 grains of black powder, a load similar to the reduced charge for the Peacemaker of later days, so it was no power-house for a shoulder gun, but it *was* quick and handy. One might say it corresponded to the misbegotten .30 caliber carbine of WW II in that it was light, generous in the magazine, and didn't kick up a fuss on discharge to fray a draftee's nerves. Another significant point is that it sold for just under $20.

In '66, Winchester improved the Henry, giving it a stronger receiver and a King-type loading port in the side. This gun took the same rim-fire cartridges and used the same brass in the receiver as its predecessor.

However, in 1873, the rifle saw some major changes. Receiver material switched from brass to iron, and a center-fire cartridge, the famous .44 W.C.F., or .44-40, was adopted. This load, as the name implies, used the .44 caliber, 200-grain bullet of the Henry but pushed it with 40 grains of powder, a distinct improvement. The resulting .44-40 cartridge, while not what anyone would consider a ferocious load today, did a lot of execution from the time it was introduced up until WW I. Whelen estimates that 70 percent of all deer killed in the U.S. in that period fell to this round.

This rifle, then, was the renowned

J. Henry & Sons U. S. Militia rifle was a .58 caliber weapon with a 35 inch barrel.

Alex Henry double barrel rifle of .450 cal.

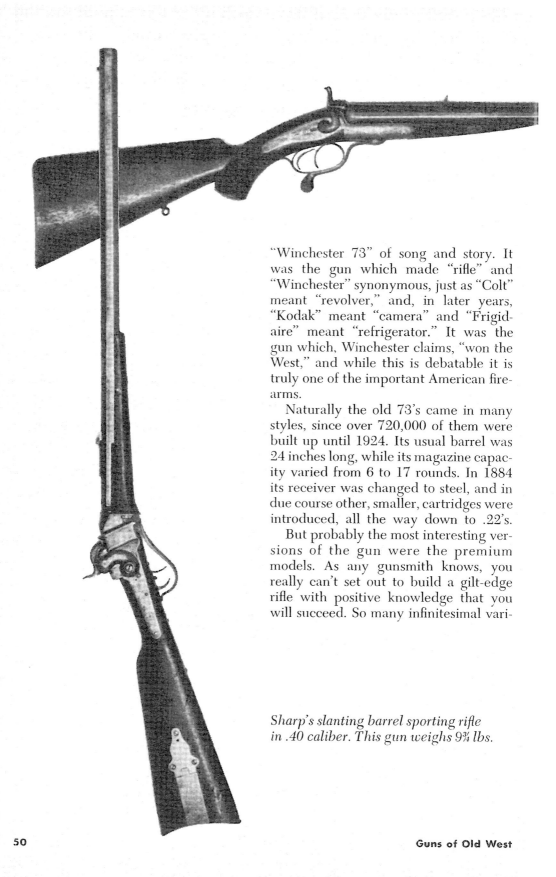

"Winchester 73" of song and story. It was the gun which made "rifle" and "Winchester" synonymous, just as "Colt" meant "revolver," and, in later years, "Kodak" meant "camera" and "Frigidaire" meant "refrigerator." It was the gun which, Winchester claims, "won the West," and while this is debatable it is truly one of the important American firearms.

Naturally the old 73's came in many styles, since over 720,000 of them were built up until 1924. Its usual barrel was 24 inches long, while its magazine capacity varied from 6 to 17 rounds. In 1884 its receiver was changed to steel, and in due course other, smaller, cartridges were introduced, all the way down to .22's.

But probably the most interesting versions of the gun were the premium models. As any gunsmith knows, you really can't set out to build a gilt-edge rifle with positive knowledge that you will succeed. So many infinitesimal vari-

Sharp's slanting barrel sporting rifle in .40 caliber. This gun weighs 9¾ lbs.

An E. M. Riley double rifle in .500 caliber.

ables affect a gun's performance that a great deal of chance is involved. A better way is to test each of a series of identical weapons and pick out those which *really* shoot. And this is just what Winchester did. In test firing all the 73's to come off the line, the top 1/10th of one percent were set aside to be restocked, engraved, usually fitted with improved sights and set triggers, and labeled "One of One-Thousand." Such guns were intended to be presentation pieces and were listed at $100 each. Again referring to relative purchasing power, this comes to a tidy sum—let's say around $600 today.

Records show that the 124 "One of 1000" rifles were good for about two minutes of the angle—a little better than today's over-the-counter hunting rifles but a good way short of our good ones. Likewise they were a bit short of the best Kentuckies at short ranges, but reached a little farther. The rainbow trajectory of the .44-40 cartridge pretty well left the 73's out of any sniping-type work, but used within their limits, on light targets at ranges below 75 yards, they were nice little guns. And they *did* keep on shooting practically forever, if that's what was needed.

It is saddening, in a sense, to note that this emphasis on proven performance in a company's product has been all but lost today. Modern manufacturers shudder at any suggestion of competitive testing for merit. They show no reluctance to claim that their newest product is the best thing ever built, but just imagine their saying, as Winchester did three-quarters of a century ago, "All our products are good, but these very few test out as better even than our highest standards can reliably produce. They are happy accidents. And you can buy them, if you want to pay the price!"

SPRINGFIELD

At the conclusion of the Civil War the U.S. Army was without question the finest in the world. Large, tough, disciplined, and vastly cagy, it was also fairly well armed. But in the last department there was room for improvement, especially after the civilian soldiers were discharged and the pros took over. The obvious need for a standardized breech loader taking a self-contained metallic cartridge was postponed by the War Department until the regular Army got down to reasonable size, whereupon the ordnance people went to work on the problem.

Winchester model 86, a .45-90, seven shot weapon.

A glance at the Henry-Winchester repeaters showed that, while they had several advantages, they were too frail for military use and could not be beefed up to take a really serious cartridge without making them far too heavy. So the decision was made to adapt the basic Minié rifle to breech loading, single-shot action.

The Allin conversion was the first successful effort in this line, utilizing a "trap-door," flip-up, breech-block containing a full-length firing pin driven by a huge, goose-neck hammer essentially the same as that of a cap-lock. The first cartridge was simply a self-contained version of the Minié round—.58 caliber with a 60-grain charge—but it became clear that breech loading permitted both a smaller bore and higher velocity so a second round was tried, a .50-70. Continuing this trend, the Army settled on .45-70 in 1873.

The first prominent success of the new equipment was the Wagon Box Fight of 1867, when a war party of Sioux under both Red Cloud and Crazy Horse set upon a military fire-wood detail. The customary tactic of the plains-Indians was the provocation of a volley from the blue-coats, followed instantly by a charge before the front-feeders could be reloaded. But the troopers at the Wagon Box all had Allin conversions and to the dismay of the Sioux they could keep up a fairly steady fire. The Indians, in spite of unusual determination and valor, were driven off with heavy losses.

The .45-70 Springfield of 1873 is one of the distinguished implements of the westward movement. By curious coincidence it appeared in the same year as two other famous weapons—the Peacemaker and the "Winchester" which made that company's name. The settlers and traders of the day liked the Winchester, but the Indian-fighting army used the Springfield. Both, of course, used Colts as well.

The "trap-door" Springfield was issued in both rifle and carbine forms. The rifle

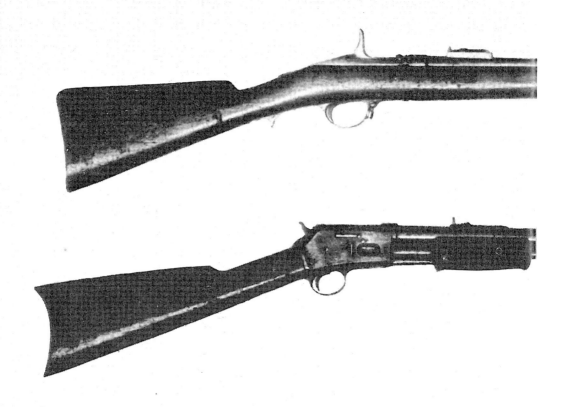

had a 32½-inch barrel and weighed 8½ lbs. The carbine had a 22-inch barrel and weighed 7 pounds. The shorter gun was equipped with a carrying ring on the left side of the receiver, designed to take the snap hook of a broad leather sling worn over the left shoulder and reaching to the right hip.

The original charge was a .405-grain bullet ahead of 70 grains of powder, to be used in both guns, but this powder charge was reduced to 55 grains for carbine use because of excessive blast in the short barrel. Since the action will hold about 25,000 p.s.i., a heavier, 500-grain bullet was found practical and issued with the 70-grain charge, in 1882. Its greater sectional density gave it better ranging qualities, as well as an increase in shock effect. Since there was now a .45-55-405 cartridge for carbines and a .45-70-500 for rifles, cases were marked

"C" or "R" on the heads to differentiate them. Either round would function safely in either weapon, but the "R" cartridge was pretty hairy to shoot in a carbine.

The Springfield '73 hit hard. Neither man nor horse needed a second shot when solidly hit. That 500-grain bullet was a considerable missile even when thrown by hand, and it left the rifle muzzle at about 1350 f/s. The 405-grain carbine bullet departed at about 1150.

Both weapons had three groove barrels with a 22 inch twist, and in spite of their six to eight pound trigger pulls, good shooting was possible with them. Since the big bullet just went on and on (it would penetrate a foot of solid pine at 400 yards) the Army developed practice courses with it out to a full 1000 yards. As the mid-range trajectory of the cartridge was some 45 *feet* at this range,

Rare U. S. Joslyn experimental rifle of the
Civil War era, a .50 caliber center-fire gun.

The Colt Lightning pump rifle, sporting
model 85, a .32-20, fifteen shot weapon.

the idea was pretty fanciful, but you *could* hit a man out there if you knew the exact distance. The bullet might slant down into him like a howitzer shell, but he wasn't any less dead for that.

It's an odd fact that the time of flight was so great at these ranges that if an adversary saw the smoke of the black powder discharge, he had time to take cover before the bullet arrived!

Marksmanship training was greatly improved during the .45-70 period, and extra pay was the reward of the "sharp-shooter," the highest category of the day. Three dollars a month extra doesn't look like much now, but when you remember that a private's full salary was $18, it's not to be sneezed at. A sharpshooter was expected to deliver six to eight inch groups from prone at 200 yards, which, with iron sights, is good with today's weapons.

Two special versions of the old Spring-field were available during its career. The Officers' Model, of 1875, was designed as a personal weapon for junior officers who had no confidence in the Colt. It was a slicked-up job with a 26 inch round barrel, a checked, pistol-grip half-stock, and a tang peep sight. These admirable guns were disposed of by the government just before WW I for exactly $2.50 each!

The target version had a six-groove octagonal barrel and took a special, long .45-80 cartridge. It also had special sights and an improved trigger action.

As a combat piece the "trap door" Springfield has been much maligned; unjustly it seems to me. This gun was standard issue throughout the Indian Wars in the West, and a careful study of the records shows that the troopers consistently outshot the Indians by an

enormous margin. Of course it may be claimed that the Indians were basically very poor marksmen, but they did live by their guns and certainly were doing their best. The ten-to-one average of the old Springfield cannot be completely discounted.

It was, of course, a rather slow weapon, especially as compared to the Winchester, but accuracy is always more desirable than volume. And when accuracy is combined with crushing power the effect is very forceful.

Extraction failure has been charged to the old gun, and there are those who claim that the Custer debacle was partly caused by it, but men who actually used the weapon in battle didn't seem to mention this in their memoirs.

A more serious drawback, which is seldom noted, was the huge size of the ammunition. Ten loose rounds weighed a pound, so a couple of bandoleers slowed even the strongest man down to a very considerable extent.

The '73 Springfield was abandoned in 1895, replaced by the .30-caliber, smokeless, magazine-fed, bolt action, high-velocity Krag. Smokeless powder was *the* great advance which made modern ballistics possible, but it didn't arrive in time to play a part in the development of the Old West.

While the Springfield was the G.I.

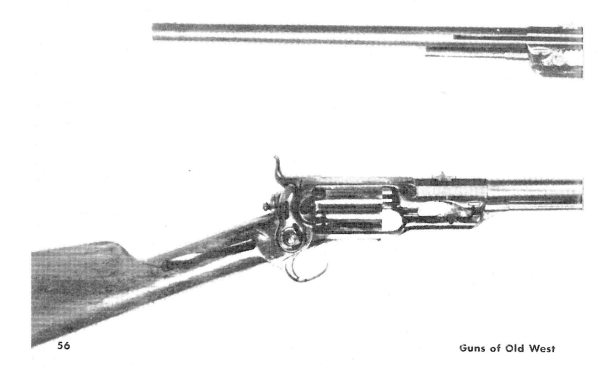

The celebrated U. S. Remington-Lee
Navy rifle. This is a .45-70, five shot gun.

weapon of the day, and the Winchester was the common civilian rifle, there was a breed of plainsman-hunter who needed something different. They wanted essentially what the Springfield offered, but improved in power, precision and long range accuracy potential.

These men turned to the Sharps rifle, a large-bore precision instrument intended mainly for buffalo hunting. The Sharps rifles featured a vertically sliding breech-block, set-triggers, precision "pin-hole" aperture sights, heavy barrels, and fine workmanship. They were also expensive.

Cartridge sizes were various, but generally larger than the Army load. .45-90 and .50-110 were popular. For obvious reasons Sharps guns were never commonplace on the frontier, but they gave excellent service when available, and most of the miraculous long shots of legend are attributed to them.

THE CHOPPERS

Any serious research into the gunplay of the Old West turns up a striking fact. The efficient gunmen of the period never went in for the foolishness of "contests" in which one man deliberately waited for another. They "outdrew" each other, not by blinding speed, *but simply by starting before the other man expected it.*

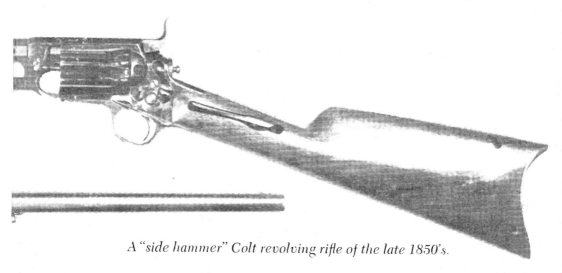

A "side hammer" Colt revolving rifle of the late 1850's.

Wyatt Earp's court testimony after the O.K. Corral affair states clearly that he challenged Tom McLowery to draw *after Earp's own gun was out and cocked.* Likewise the whole Earp faction had their guns in their hands before they came within range of the Clanton-McLowery group.

This is not to say that the old gunslingers *couldn't* do fancywork in the leatherslapping line, but that they regarded it strictly as a desperate measure to be used only after they had made the dire mistake of not anticipating action.

Now to follow up on this theory, we find that none of the real killers of the day actually regarded his Colt as his *primary* weapon. He wore it, of course, all the time, since no one could tell for sure when trouble might arise, but if he *knew* there was going to a fight, his sixgun was his secondary battery.

Think back for a moment. What did Bill Hickok carry as he patrolled the streets of Abilene? What did Doc Hol-

liday carry slung under his arm on those occasions when he expected a fight? What did the terrible John Slaughter use when the famous Mexican bandit Chacon came looking for him? What did every stage coach guard carry across his lap as he waited for ambush? What did Earp himself—television's own idea of a pistolero—use when he held back the lynch mob shouting for the life of Johnny-Behind-the-Deuce?

In each case the answer is the deadliest close combat weapon known in that day or this—a shotgun!

A word of advice. If you know someone is coming to kill you, and you don't want to run away, forget that pistol and grab a shotgun! If you're a police officer and you have to go into a building after an armed hoodlum who doesn't want to be taken alive—use a shotgun! If you're a householder in a tough neighborhood and you hear strange company downstairs after the family is asleep for the night, investigate with a shotgun!

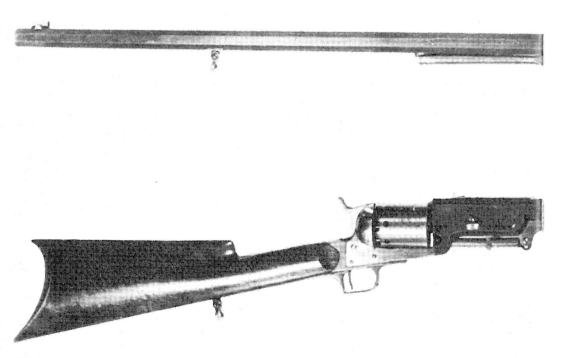

A load of buckshot from a large bore shotgun at short range behaves on a human being much like a load of bird shot centered on a quail—it's conclusive!

In addition, it's so easy to hit with! A pistol is a somewhat tricky weapon to use well without extensive experience, but you can hardly miss with a shotgun. It's two-hand pointing and spreading charge make it about as difficult to use as a garden hose—and even if you miss with the first charge, the second is ready without any action on your part.

The gunmen of the Old West didn't have the repeaters we have today, so they used doubles, nearly always with exposed hammers and often front-feeders. Ten gage was the popular bore size in both breech and muzzle loaders, and about 12 #0 buckshot (.32 caliber round balls) was the usual load.

A man doesn't stand up to such a weapon at short range, unless he's insane, because he has no chance against it. And the frontier lawmen intended it

that way. Those who gave their adversaries a chance died, and that ended their ideas of chivalry.

The barrels of shotguns intended strictly for combat use were normally cut to about 20 inches, shorter if they were to be carried concealed. Holliday's famous chopper had barrels about 14 inches long. Hickok, however, generally used full-length, fowling-type barrels, claiming that he had no need to conceal the gun and that the long tubes gave better patterns. ("Choking" of shotgun muzzles was not used then.)

One weapon which seems a natural to me has never turned up in my research —at least it has never been mentioned as figuring in any significant fight. This is the Colt revolving shotgun in .75 caliber (just over 12 gage) and cut down for combat. This was a five-shot repeater —it could even, I imagine, be fanned! There, it would appear, was just what the doctor (Holliday, that is) *should* have ordered. ■

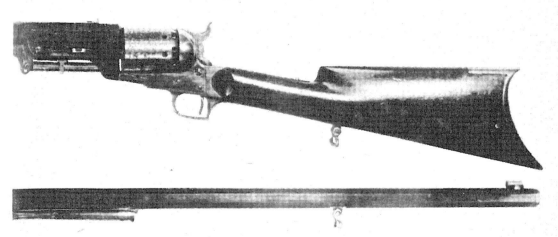

A Colt revolving rifle of Paterson vintage.

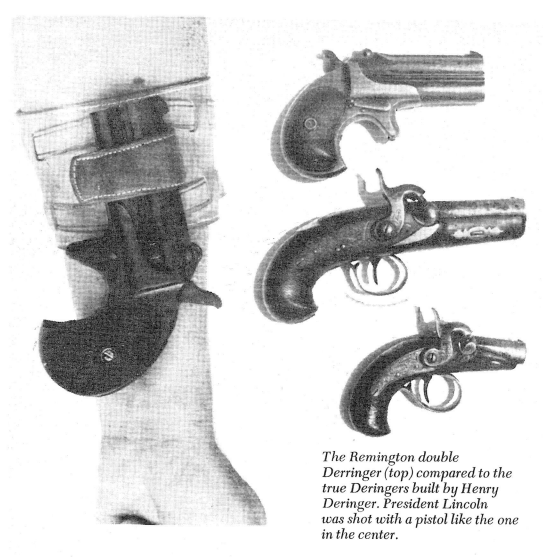

The Remington double
Derringer (top) compared to the
true Deringers built by Henry
Deringer. President Lincoln
was shot with a pistol like the one
in the center.

*The Derringer, above in a wrist holder;
below, as finely engraved thing of beauty.*

TO get power sufficient to give reliable protection against men, you have to carry a big sidearm. This is true today, but in the early days of the west it was even more so, for black powder and low tensile steels made bulk essential to power.

However, there has always been a need for a concealable handgun, small enough and light enough to be worn continuously without any indication that the wearer was armed. The desirability of a hideout gun to the criminal element is obvious, but we should remember also that lawmen and various sorts of plainclothes agents frequently need to be armed without appearing so.

The problem is that reducing size to

The Little Ones

any appreciable extent also reduces efficiency to a point where it is all but lost, and practically limits the weapon to use as a threat only. Since little guns *can* kill, they serve a valid purpose in this way. The fact that they *probably* won't doesn't make it easier on your nerves when one is pointed at your middle.

The pocket guns of the Old West came in three general forms, the first and best known of which was the Derringer. There's a little elementary confusion about this name since Henry Deringer (one "r") designed and produced a small, single-shot muzzle-loading, large-bore, cap-lock pistol long before William Elliot designed the small, double-barreled, breech-loading, large-bore, car-

tridge pistol known as the Derringer (two "r's"). Both guns were widely used, but the Deringer was built by Deringer himself prior to the Civil War, while the Derringer was built by Remington afterward.

Both pistols were hideout guns which attempted to achieve efficiency by means of a large (.41") bore size. The round ball of the muzzle loader weighed about 100 grains while the conical bullet of the rim-fire cartridge weighed 130. But the charge was so light in either case that velocity was very low—around 500 f/s—and stopping power was not great—quite poor, as a matter of fact. In addition, the combination of relatively large diameter with low velocity produced

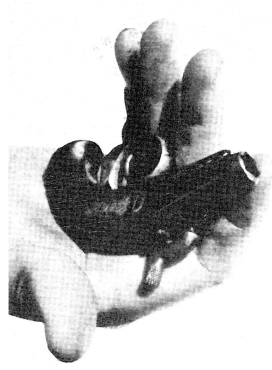

A vest pocket Derringer of pre-Civil War vintage. Note the large (.41) bore of this gun.

very little penetration. A well filled wallet or a brawny arm could stop it.

The chief danger from either gun was infection. The greased lead bullet of the rim-fire round picked up all sorts of trash, and tended to punch a wad of unsanitary textiles into the target's midsection without pushing it out the other side.

Booth used a Deringer to shoot Lincoln and we all know what a messy job that was.

The Remington Double Derringer was marketed in 1866, and nearly 160,000 were eventually produced, a testimonial to the need for a hideout gun, but I think a large measure of the weapon's popularity was the naive equation of bore-size with power in the public mind.

The second type of stingy gun was the toy revolver, a tiny item of .22 to .32 caliber of which several are illustrated. These must be regarded purely as threat-weapons. Their entire value was moral, since nobody wants to be shot, even with a toy.

And the third class of pocket pistol

Two brass frame pocket Colts of 1880's.

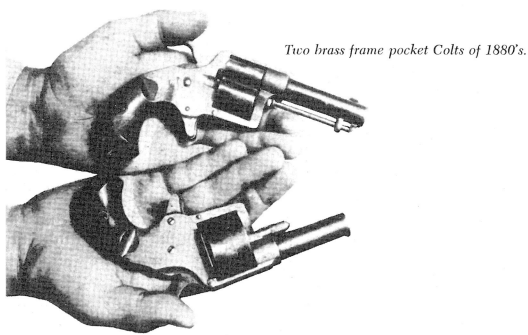

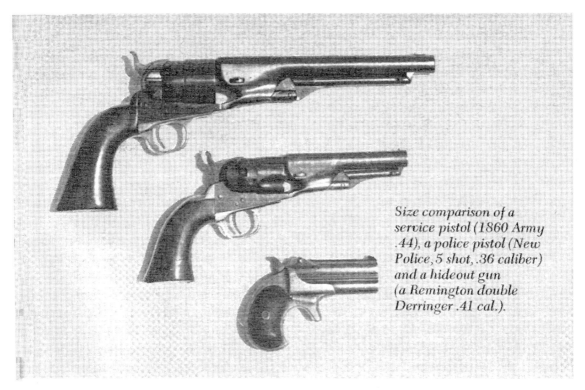

Size comparison of a service pistol (1860 Army .44), a police pistol (New Police, 5 shot, .36 caliber) and a hideout gun (a Remington double Derringer .41 cal.).

was the five-shot "police" revolver, of .36″ caliber in cap-and-ball form, and .38 when cartridges were introduced. These were practical guns, for while they weren't really powerful enough to be safe, they provided compensating qualities of reduced size and weight. The Colt "Wells Fargo" was such a gun, and enough success was achieved with the type to lead our military authorities along an unsatisfactory small-caliber trend until after the Philippine Wars. ■

Hideout guns of the gunfighter era. Top is famed Remington double Derringer, compared for size with Colt pocket .32. The .41 rim fire cartridge of the Derringer was more effective, but not nearly the man-stopper you often hear about.

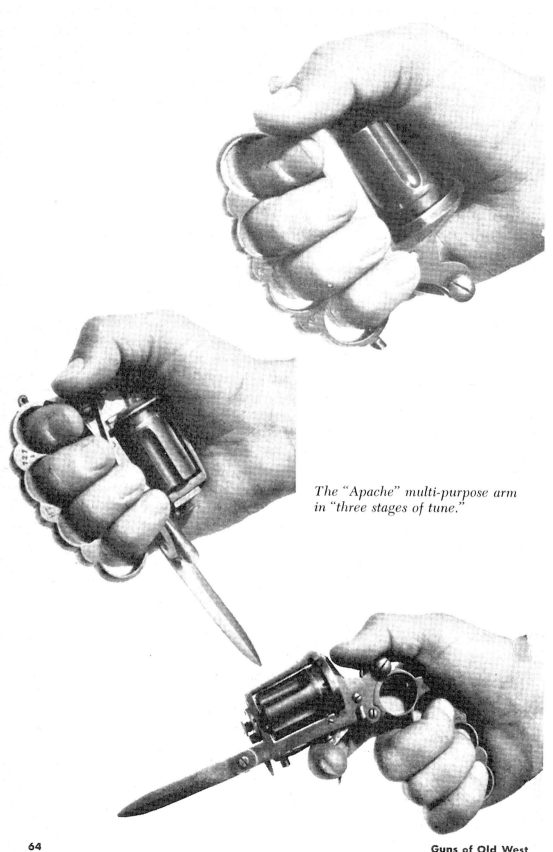

The "Apache" multi-purpose arm in "three stages of tune."

Guns of Old West